KU-286-720

TALES TOLD BY FOSSILS:
UNEARTHING LIFE'S PAST

What are fossils?

Fossils are the remains or traces of things
that lived during past geologic times and
were buried in rocks of the earth's crust.
There the ancient organisms lay until rains,
rivers, rock slides, power shovels, or
collectors' picks brought them to light again.
The tale told by these fossils began 1600 to
2700 million years ago.

3 cde

Also by Carroll Lane Fenton

TALES TOLD BY FOSSILS:
FROM DINOSAURS TO MAN

and published by CAROUSEL BOOKS

Tales Told by Fossils: Unearthing Life's Past

CARROLL LANE FENTON

Originally published with
TALES TOLD BY FOSSILS: FROM DINOSAURS TO MAN
in one volume entitled TALES TOLD BY FOSSILS

CAROUSEL EDITOR: ANNE WOOD

TRANSWORLD PUBLISHERS LTD

TALES TOLD BY FOSSILS: UNEARTHING LIFE'S PAST
A CAROUSEL BOOK 0 552 54046 3

Originally published in Great Britain with
TALES TOLD BY FOSSILS: FROM DINOSAURS TO MAN
in one volume entitled TALES TOLD BY FOSSILS
by The World's Work (1913) Ltd.

PRINTING HISTORY
The World's Work edition published 1967
The World's Work edition second impression 1968
Carousel edition published 1974

Copyright ©1966 by Carroll Lane Fenton
Chapter 10 only Copyright ©1967 by The World's Work (1913) Ltd.

Conditions of sale — This book is sold subject to the condition that it
shall not, by way of trade or otherwise, be lent, re-sold, hired out or
otherwise circulated without the publisher's prior consent in any form
of binding or cover other than that in which it is published and
without a similar condition including this condition being imposed on the
subsequent purchaser.

Carousel Books are published by
Transworld Publishers Ltd., Cavendish House,
57-79 Uxbridge Road, Ealing, London W5.

Printed by James Paton Ltd., Paisley, Scotland

CONTENTS

Page

Introduction 8

1 Unearthing Life's Past 9

2 What Fossils Reveal 15

3 Building Earth's Time Scale 25

4 Shells, Sea-mud, and Mountains 32

5 Skin-crusted Trilobites 43

6 The Repetitive Horn-shells .... 5(

7 Stalks and Stars 63

8 From Fins to Legs and Land 73

9 Life and Death on Deltas 83

10 Museums and Books 91

Glossary 97

Index with pronunciations 105

PUBLISHERS NOTE

This edition of *Tales Told by Fossils* has been reproduced from the original American edition. It consequently follows the American spelling and numerical conventions in which one billion equals one thousand millions (1,000,000,000).

Chapter 10, Museums and Books, has been rewritten for this edition to give the reader in the British Isles and the Commonwealth an extensive list of places where more information on this subject may be found.

The TIME SCALE follows the American terminology. A European TIME SCALE would call 'Epoch' a 'Period' and would not divide the CARBONIFEROUS PERIOD into the 'Pennsylvanian Period' and the 'Mississippian Period'.

ABOUT FACTS AND ILLUSTRATIONS

Though this is not a large book, it ranges the world of fossils from early algae to dinosaurs and men. (Volumn Two) . It therefore goes far beyond the author's field work and research. The author is indebted to many scientists on whose publications he has relied for facts beyond his own experience.

Most of the illustrations in Chapters 1-10 have been taken or adapted from *The Fossil Book*, by C. L. and M. A. Fenton (Doubleday & Company, 1958). Again, many sources have been drawn upon. Especially important have been restorations of reptiles and mammals by the late Charles R. Knight and R. Bruce Horsfall, who worked principally with scientists of the American Museum of Natural History and Princeton University.

INTRODUCTION

In this volume of *TALES TOLD BY FOSSILS* the story of life during ancient geologic times has been traced from the Precambrian era, over 2700 million years ago, and traces the development of life up until the Permian Period, 280 million years ago.

In the second volume — *TALES TOLD BY FOSSILS: From Dinosaurs to Man* — the story continues with the late Triassic Period, 230 million years ago, and lizard-hipped dinosaurs, up until 100,000 years ago and Neanderthal man.

1 UNEARTHING LIFE'S PAST

ONE DAY IN 1897, a young man named Walter Granger rode across a plain in southeastern Wyoming. Far south of him rose a ridge known as Como Bluff; northward the land dipped into a shallow valley, or "draw," that led to the Little Medicine Bow River. At the head of the draw stood a half-ruined cabin built by a sheep herder. Ground around it was littered with rusty-brown boulders.

Granger was collecting fossils for the then-young American Museum of Natural History, in New York City. He soon saw that the boulders were more than lumps of stone; they were battered, weather-beaten bones of big dinosaurs. Other bones, not so badly worn, formed the lower walls of the cabin. All had come from shaly sandstone that formed the surrounding land.

The collector examined both boulders and sandstone; then he reported that Bone Cabin Draw contained a rich deposit of dinosaurian fossils. Collecting began the following spring, and Granger soon found the right hind leg of a reptile whose limbs had been unknown. Work continued through six summers, into the autumn of 1903. By that time the Bone Cabin deposit had yielded 483 portions of varied dinosaurs, as well as remains of turtles and crocodiles. These specimens formed the greatest collection of fossil reptile remains ever taken from a single locality.

But before we go further, what are fossils?

We frequently think of fossils as prehistoric plants and animals that have been "turned into stone," or petrified. Many fossils are not stony, however, and many that are have not been petrified. An acceptable definition must provide for both types, and it should do more than tell us that

fossils lived before human beings learned to write down
facts of history or carve them on stone. That first happened
about 5300 years ago, but most fossils are so much more
than 5300 years old that their great antiquity should be indicated.

Some inclusive definitions are long, but these demands
can be met without wordiness or technicality. An adequate
definition says that *fossils are remains or traces of things that
lived during ancient geologic times and were buried in rocks
that settled on the earth's outer portion, or crusts.* This statement will serve us well if we bear in mind three facts:

First, *ancient geologic times* began with the earliest ages
that can be traced in rocks and extended through the epoch
that directly followed the last great Ice Age. In years, this
means from perhaps 3,500,000,000 to about 10,000 B.C. As
yet, however, few fossils have been found in rocks more
than 1800 million years old.

Second, *rocks* are not necessarily *stones*. Most rocks that
covered ancient plants and animals were soil, sand, mud, or

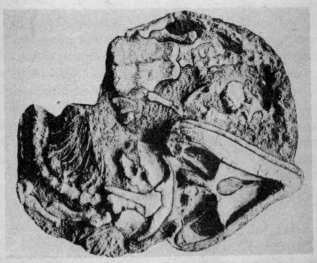

Remains of a reptile from the Permian Red Beds of Texas. These bones are
exceptionally well preserved.

other loose materials. Many of these have become hard stones, but some are almost as far from being solid as they ever were. Countless fossils lie in sands or clays that crumble in our hands though they are 20, 40, or even 440 million years old.

Third, most scientists who write about very ancient men use the word "fossilized" to mean *petrified*. When one of these authors says that a skull has not been fossilized he means only that it has not become stony. It still may be old enough to rank as a fossil.

Some rocks have changed little; others have solidified or have been remade. Similarly, some fossils are much as they were when they were alive, others retain only a little once-living material, and many have none at all. Some shells, for example, still show colour patterns; ancient mammoths that were frozen in icy ground retain their flesh, skin, and hair. Many leaves, however, are thin films of carbon that remained after most of their original substance had decayed. Other leaves are mere impressions left in soft mud or sand which then hardened. Footprints are impressions, too, but most fossil burrows are solidified sand that filled holes dug by worms and other small animals.

All these, however, are less abundant than petrified remains. Most of the latter are shells or other hard coverings, but many are bones or wood. They have been filled or replaced by stony material that may be harder than the rock around them. This explains why petrified fossils often "weather out" and lie on the ground while rocks that once covered them disappear.

Collecting Fossils

Though fossils have been preserved in many ways, each of them tells its part in the story of life during ancient geologic times. It is to discover this story that museums and individuals collect and study fossils. Big ones are brought in by expeditions; to dig up and pack a dinosaur or mammoth is a job for many hands. Seven skilled collectors and scientists worked at Bone Cabin in 1899, with help from pick-and-shovel men and teamsters. An expedition to Asia, for plants, animals, and rocks, as well as for fossils, had a staff of scientists, technicians, artists, photographers, mechanics, and even camel drivers, since camel trains carried petrol for trucks and passenger cars. Hair pulled from the camels as they shed was used in packing specimens.

Large expeditions have made great discoveries, but small ones are important, too. Many fine skeletons have been found by three or four men on horseback, with a wagon for camp gear and specimens. Today, a Jeep takes the place of horses, and one truck does the work of several wagons.

Most expeditions go far afield; individual collectors usually work near home. They do so because they have limited time, and because fossil beds often lie in the midst of civilization. Ravines close to Minneapolis, for example, have been worn through beds that contain ancient snails and clams, as well as other marine creatures. Sea shells are common in Cincinnati, where they lie on every hillside and in almost every ditch. Corals weather out of shaly pastures in western New York; crinoids, or sea lilies, are found in quarries where limestone is crushed as fertilizer for Iowa cornfields. Bones of Ice-age mammals underlie a park in Los Angeles.

Ice-age Angeleños include mammoths and giant lions; 45-foot reptiles once swam where suburbs now stand in New Jersey; bones of ground sloths 10 feet long have been dug from farms in Ohio. But such oversized creatures are exceptions, for most fossils within reach of home-based collectors are small. Even the white sharks of ancient Maryland are not big fossils; though the fish once were 40 to 50 feet long, their only remains are petrified teeth 4 to 8 inches in length.

Small size, however, does not mean that a fossil is unimportant. The oldest known plants are so tiny that they can be seen only through a microscope, and few corals, shells, or sea lilies are big. Indeed, specimens less than 6 inches in length tell most of life's story during its first 1300 million years. Even when large plants and animals became common, small species outnumbered giants by many thousands to one.

Besides being more plentiful than big ones, small fossils are easier to handle. We realize this when we see how two collectors obtain and "prepare" their specimens.

The first collector is out for ancient sea shells and corals. For an hour or two he works on slabs of limestone, splitting them with a chisel and a geologist's pick. When he finds a fossil, he breaks it out, taking care to leave some rock around it. After wrapping it in newspaper, he puts the specimen into his knapsack or a carton.

Above the limestone are layers of shale which rains have reduced to clay. Here the collector stoops low or crawls, picking up specimens that lie on the surface and prying others out of the ground. Most of these go into paper bags; those that are especially delicate are wrapped in tissue paper or cotton and placed in small boxes or wide-mouthed bottles. Tiny fossils that are abundant may be scooped up or swept into bags with a whisk broom.

When this collector returns to his laboratory or basement workroom, he chips excess rock from the fossils that were found in limestone. Those from shale are washed to soften their coating of clay; any that still clings to them is removed with a stiff brush, a needle, or a knife. If the fossils are delicate, this work may be done under a magnifier.

The second collector, who is seeking big vertebrates, may begin by spying the tip of a bone that projects from shale or sandstone. With his pick he uncovers a few more bones; if they show that the fossil is worth taking out, he removes just enough rock to show where it lies and where he must dig to obtain it without damage. Only after this has been done can he begin to remove his specimens.

This requires skill and great care, for even the hardest petrified bones seldom are very strong. Our collector of vertebrates must know when to change from pick or crowbar to chisel; when to lay the chisel aside in favour of scraper and brush. He works till he knows where his specimen ends; then he cuts a trench around it and removes the rock beneath. As he does so, assistants set up a small derrick and equip it with block and tackle. With them the collector and his helpers will lift rock and fossil out of the ground.

Here we get ahead of the story—much too far ahead. As bone after bone is exposed, it is covered with tissue paper and soaked with shellac or some chemical preservative. Cracks may be cemented; splints of wood or steel are placed upon weak or shattered blocks of stone. Strips of cloth dipped in wet plaster of Paris are then spread over splints, fossil, and rock, crossing and recrossing until the mass is rigidly bound together. Not until the plaster hardens can the fossil be raised and boxed for shipment.

When box and contents reach the museum, the splints and bandages are removed. Skilled preparators then cut away excess rock, working first with small hammers and chisels, and finally with dentists' drills. Bones that still are intact need only be cleaned; those shattered since they became fossils are pieced together bit by bit and then are put away for study or are assembled into skeletons. These, in turn, must be supported by plaster and bars or tubes of metal so they can be displayed.

Sometimes this process must be reversed, and skeletons that have been "mounted" are taken down for study or repair. Sometimes, too, bones that have been assembled from fragments are then separated for examination. The results may suggest skulls or vertebrae of modern animals that have been taken apart for anatomical study. But no modern skull is as hard to take apart as one that has been in the ground for millions upon millions of years.

2   WHAT FOSSILS REVEAL

FOSSILS RECORD the story of life during past ages. But is that record adequate? Do fossils give the facts we need to construct a reliable, well-rounded account?

Some critics who ask these questions give a negative reply. Most fossil animals, they say, are merely petrified hard parts: bones, shells, or crustlike coats from which all living material has vanished. Petrified wood is no better; moreover, most ancient plants are known from leaves which are either black films of carbon or impressions in sandstone or shale. Some reptiles survive only as footprints, and worms have been described from solidified sand that filled their burrows. Such fossils do not even show the shapes of creatures that made them.

With some exceptions these statements are true; no one who works with fossils denies them. It is equally true that most of the things that lived during past ages did not become fossils when they died. Countless creatures without hard parts decayed; so did the vast majority of seaweeds and soft, herbaceous land-plants. Fish and four-footed animals met the same fate unless their remains were soon covered by fine sand or mud. Creatures of rocky seashores vanished as waves smashed their shells into bits too small for recognition. Waves also destroyed tracks and burrows, and shifting rivers swept away many footprints that had been left on muddy sand.

Fossils are the remains and traces that escaped this wholesale destruction. No one can estimate their number, but they must be only a tiny fraction of the total that lived and died during the past two billion years. This fact, like the imperfection of remains and traces that were preserved, seems to support the critics who say that fossils really tell

1 and 2 are sections cut through fossil corals; they show structures built by the creatures' soft bodies; 3, the interior of a lamp-shell, bears the "scars" to which muscles were attached.

very little of life's story during the long geologic past.

Still, the record is much better than words alone imply. It is true that hordes of ancient organisms lived, died, and disappeared—but it is equally true that other hordes were buried in rocks and became fossils. Limy algae fill beds 10 to 100 feet thick that extend across scores of miles. Coral banks are quite as extensive; oysterlike shells are so abundant that collectors gather hundreds in a day. With very small fossils the number increases to thousands, and even big fossils are not always rare. Visitors to the Petrified Forest, in northern Arizona, may climb one hillock and look down on hundreds of stony logs. In Montana, one collector found remains of some 500 skulls that belonged to a single type of dinosaur.

Not only are many fossils abundant; they exist in great variety. Among plants they range from the simplest algae to trees and highly specialized grasses. Animals range from sponges to whales among sea-dwellers, and from worms to human beings on land. There is also a vast array of one-celled creatures called protozoans, which seem to belong to several kingdoms distinct from both plants and animals.

Most of these fossils are petrified—but instead of being meaningless fragments, they are often preserved in amazing and very meaningful detail. Many skeletons contain almost every bone. A fossil coral may look like a stone, but its interior is an orderly maze of ridges and plates arranged in a pattern which shows the nature and relationships of the soft-

Carbonized fossils of Middle Cambrian age, perhaps 550 million years old. Number 1, a marine worm, preserves the shape of the body and spines on its surface; 2 is a wormlike creature with skin, head, spines, and legs; 3, a relative of the trilobites, shows both shape and internal organs.

bodied animal that made them. Ancient shells reveal the fibres and grains of which they are made, as well as ridges, frills, spines, and bosses on their surfaces. Cell walls are preserved in much petrified wood, as well as in a surprising number of ferns and small herbaceous plants. There also are threadlike fungi so small that their nature is hardly apparent until they are greatly magnified.

Such details are lacking from films of carbon and impressions in sandstone or shale. Yet impressions show the shapes and veins of leaves as clearly as do modern plants that are pressed and kept for scientific study. Impressions of shells, small skulls, and bones are so clear that they can be reproduced in plaster or modelling compounds and examined almost as if they were petrified. Many fossil insects and spiders also are impressions, as are wing membranes of flying reptiles and feathers of the earliest birds. Dinosaur "Mummies" contain petrified bones, but their rough skins are impressions in sand that covered the sun-dried carcasses and hardened into stone. Virtually all fossil jellyfish are imprints, yet they show organs in the once-watery bodies. They also are exceptions to the rule that animals without hard parts have not become fossils.

Most carbonized fossils show little more than impressions. But marine reptiles from Europe and fish from northern Ohio preserve carbonized shapes of bodies and fins, as well as skin that sometimes is darker on the sides and back than it is below. Much older fossils from the Canadian Rockies include carbonized seaweeds, small "shellfish" whose digestive systems show plainly, and worms with fleshy snouts and hooked or bristly spines. Soft-bodied parasitic flatworms have been found in carbonized insects.

The complaint that petrified fossils preserve only hard parts must also be qualified. Whole fairy shrimps and spiders have been found, as well as insects, slugs, a reptile head complete with eyes, and even the fleshy breast of a bird. The fairy shrimps, which are fresh-water crustaceans, include females whose pouches are full of eggs. Some insects show well-preserved muscles and minute tubes that once carried air through the bodies. Other insects include pupae and softbodied caterpillars as well as adults.

Even these fossils are surpassed by some spiders in amber and spores in cannel coal. The former preserve leg muscles, internal organs, and cells in the body wall; silk spun 30 million years ago still leads from spinnerets. Spores, which are reproductive cells of plants such as ferns, contain nuclei that served as centres of life when the cells were jellylike protoplasm. In some nuclei are chromosomes whose beadlike sections once were clusters of genes, the particles which would have determined both hereditary structure and appearance had the spores lived to become new plants.

The most nearly perfect large fossils are those of mammoths that were frozen in ground ice of Siberia and Alaska. They include bones, tendons, flesh, skin, and dried blood; half-chewed food lies between the teeth and partly digested meals fill the stomachs. Such remains are much more revealing than the dried carcasses and deposits of dung that are sometimes found in desert caves.

Still fossils need not include hair or soft parts in order to give information about them. Varied bivalves, for example, bear scars made by muscles that closed or opened the shells. Channels show where watery blood flowed through flesh; curved lines record the position of tubes that brought food into ancient clams. Bones show that some reptiles had paddle-shaped flippers, though the legs of other reptiles looked like fins.

Among vertebrates, most muscles are fastened to bones. Marks on petrified bones show the positions, shapes, and sizes of muscles that operated parts ranging from tails and legs to jaws. When these muscles are restored on paper or in modelling clay, they reveal the proportions of ancient animals, the attitudes they could assume, and movements that could be made by head, neck, and legs. Such evidence is the basis of reconstructions which show fossil vertebrates as they looked while they were alive.

Skulls reveal the size, shape, and structure of brains, as well as nerves that once led from them. In fact, we have a surprising amount of information about the sensory, mental, and motor equipment of creatures ranging from armoured pre-fish to men. Some fishlike agnaths, for example, felt heat and cold and heard low sounds by means of nerve-endings distributed along channels, or canals, that crisscrossed bony armour on the head and forward part of the body. Cavities holding the brains of flying reptiles show that these creatures had a poor sense of smell but were able to see very well. Big dinosaurs had such large bodies and such small, inefficient brains that their legs and tails were largely controlled by greatly enlarged nerve-knots, or ganglia, between the shoulders and above the hips. The earliest men, who ranged from Africa to Europe and across Asia, possessed small skulls with low foreheads, which show that their brains were neither as large nor as efficient as ours. Still, these poor brains seem to have furnished the mental requirements for speech.

All living things grow, and many change greatly as they do so. Series of petrified skulls and skin-crusts trace the development of several ancient animals from larvae or unhatched eggs to adults. One famous series of skulls traces growth of the head in horned dinosaurs -whose partly developed eggs were found in what is now Mongolia.

Series of petrified shells form similar records, but snails, clams, and lamp-shells (or brachiopods) preserved changes in size, shape, and surface ornamentation on their individual shells. Thus a snail that began by covering its body with a smooth, twisted cap soon added a coil with cross ribs and then built whorls with spiral ridges. Last came a narrow channel that extended far forward, covering a fleshy tube that took water into the body. Lines formed when growth stopped for a while show how both clams and brachiopods changed shape as they grew up and then became old. On many shells, these changes were accompanied by new types of ornamentation.

Accidents and disease were common in the past, just as they are today. Some petrified trees show partly healed burns; bones and shells contain healed breaks; legs and even parts of the body were bitten from turtles and from jointed animals very distantly related to crabs. Logs bear lumps caused by fungus and other diseases; bones reveal tumours, abscesses, inflammation of the marrow, and the results of rheumatism and arthritis. Ancient men suffered from tuberculosis of the spine, rheumatism, ulcerated teeth and jaws, and infected wounds.

Fossils also reveal the surroundings, or environments, of ancient organisms. Trees undoubtedly lived on land, but seaweeds must have grown in salt water. All living corals, scallops, and whales are marine; we infer that their fossil relatives also lived in seas and oceans. On the other hand, fossils related to living fresh-water fish, snails, and mussels are assigned to ancient streams, lakes, and ponds. Ice-age mastodons often waded into swamps while feeding, for their bones are now found where they were mired. Ancient ground sloths were just what their name says, for their size (some were 20 feet long) shows that they could not live in trees, as their modern relatives do.

Many fossils record the climatic conditions under which they lived. Woolly mammoths whose carcasses lie in ground ice plainly experienced a climate as cold as that of central Siberia today. Big dinosaurs, on the other hand, could live only where warm weather lasted the year round. Palms and breadfruit trees required warm to tropical climates, and their fossils in Spitsbergen and Greenland mean that those regions were virtually tropical. Coal-age trees probably needed less heat, but their lack of annual rings is evidence that all seasons were essentially alike.

A variety of evidence shows how ancient animals behaved. Slim sharks must have been swift swimmers, but skates spent most of their time on the bottom, eating creatures which they found in sand or mud. Specimens with impressions of flesh show that fossils known as belemnoids looked, swam, and caught prey like present-day squids. When a squid is attacked, it ejects a cloud of inky liquid that seems to blind enemies. It really paralyses their organs of smell, so they cannot follow their intended victim. Ink bags in fossils show that belemnoids also used this method of defence.

Ancient barnacles, as well as oysters and molluscs related to them, often attached themselves to shells. Clams of several kinds burrowed into sunken logs, in which their fossils are found today. Some snails crawled in sand as they hunted for food; the marks they left are easily told from the work of worms that swallowed mud or sand, digested whatever food it contained, and left the refuse behind as they burrowed. These fossils also differ from those made by worms which cast leftover mud on the sea bottom, much as modern earthworms leave castings on land.

A honeycomb coral preserves structures
built as the animals grew.

Interior of a mollusc shell, showing marks
made by muscles and other soft parts.

Veins as well as shape appear in this
impression of a sycamore leaf.

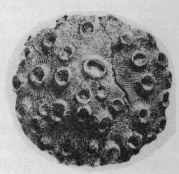

A colonial coral, showing ridges built
by the individual animals.

Several modern snails bore holes into other snails or clams, insert a rasping tongue, and devour their victims alive. Similar borings are found in fossils ranging from 2 to 430 million years in age. Other snails clung to the tops of sea lilies, or crinoids, and fed upon the wastes of their hosts. The petrified shells fit the crinoids to which some are still attached.

These snails took their food as it came, but many vertebrates were active hunters. Carnivorous dinosaurs followed victims by walking or running on their hind legs—only footprints of hind feet are preserved, and petrified bones show that the forelegs were too short to reach the ground. Some of these creatures left broken teeth among the

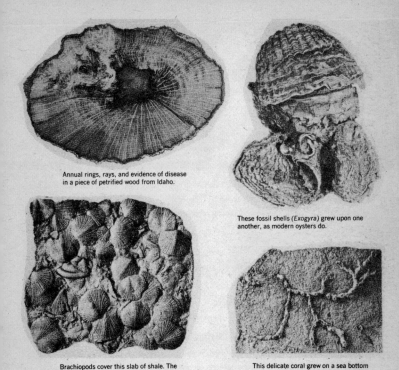

Annual rings, rays, and evidence of disease in a piece of petrified wood from Idaho.

These fossil shells (*Exogyra*) grew upon one another, as modern oysters do.

Brachiopods cover this slab of shale. The arrow points to a boring made by a snail.

This delicate coral grew on a sea bottom of fine, hard mud that settled very slowly.

bones of their prey, and at least one carnivore stepped into the footprints of an herbivore which it was stalking. Herbivores fed on plants—but petrified stomach contents show that at least one plant-eating dinosaur also swallowed bony animals. Perhaps it got them without knowing, as it gulped leaves.

Several marine reptiles and fish swallowed food whole, for the undigested remains have been found. A few fish choked to death when meals stuck in their throats; others apparently were killed by their victims' final struggles. That seems to have been the fate of one 14-foot relative of the tarpon, for it died soon after swallowing a fish 5 feet 7 inches in length. But a reptile seemingly swam away and sought other food after

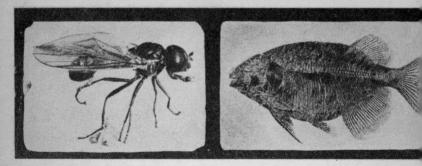

The fly in amber (left) shows hairs on the legs and facets in the eyes.
(Photo by F. M. .Carpenter) The fossil fish (right) preserves an
outline of the body as well as hundreds of small bones.

biting into the shell of a creature distantly related to the
modern nautilus.

Some animals never leave their own home ranges, but
many strong swimmers travel long distances. About 80
million years ago, a marine reptile swallowed some pink
pebbles in the region where Minnesota, Iowa, and South
Dakota now meet. The creature then swam at least 400 miles,
for his petrified bones—and the pink pebbles—were
discovered in western Kansas.

There is no reason to think that this reptile followed an
established pattern when it swam to what now is Kansas. But
"devils' corkscrews" of northwestern Nebraska tell a
different story. These fossils are hardened fillings of burrows
dug by land-dwelling beavers; each filling is a spiral that goes
several feet into the ground and then becomes an upward-
slanting tunnel with a slightly enlarged sleeping chamber at
the end. The whole structure seems to represent an inherited
pattern like the one that leads fiddler crabs of today's Pacific
coast to dig deep burrows with one or two branches ending in
small chambers. It is hardly too much to call the devil's
corkscrew the fossilized instinct of an animal that lived some
15 million years ago.

3 BUILDING EARTH'S TIME SCALE

LET US NOW return to the hill where a collector is getting invertebrate fossils from limestone and shale. These rocks lie in layers and beds, or strata, in the order in which they were formed. The first and oldest bed, therefore, is found at the bottom; the latest and youngest appears at the top. Our collector gathers his fossils in this order and labels them according to the beds from which they were taken. If he likes, he may arrange them in a series that will record the history of animals while rocks in the hill were accumulating.

This history will not be long, for the hill is not very high. The record may also fit only one region, for rocks settled in different surroundings and at different times in varied areas. Still, series can be pieced together—not merely from one place to another, but from continent to continent and through deposits of all the ages during which plants, animals, and other organisms have become plentiful fossils. The result, extended by facts obtained from rocks, is a time scale of life's—and earth's—history that embraces more than 3000 million years.

This use of fossils to build a time scale depends on two principles that have been tested for more than 150 years. The first principle states that living things changed with the passing of time, so that some fossils of any period or epoch differ from those of every other. The second principle reverses the first; since fossils differ in rocks of different ages, rocks that contain similar fossils formed at about the same time.

With a diagram, we can use these rules to build up part of our scale. Each column in the diagram represents the rocks exposed in a single slope, hillside, or quarry. Each column, or geologic section, is divided in part by the nature of its rocks, but chiefly by *index fossils* which are found in different beds or formations. Because space is limited, our diagram shows only one index fossil in each bed.

No section duplicates any other, but sections do overlap. At the top of Section 1, for example, beds of limestone contain a sea urchin that also appears in Sections 2, 3, and 7. We therefore match, or correlate, these beds of limestone as well as the shale that lies below them.

Above the limestone in Sections 2, 3 and 7 lie cross-bedded sandstones which seem to belong to a single formation. Section 2 shows that they do, for in it the sandstones are covered by beds which there, as well as in Section 7, contain shells related to oysters. Shells of a different type enable us to correlate the fifth bed in Section 7 with one near the base of Section 4. Other shells permit us to match beds in Sections 5 and 6 and so complete our composite section, which extends from the bottom of Section 1 to the top of 6.

This, too is a limited series, which formed during a small portion of the earth's history. But by matching fossils the

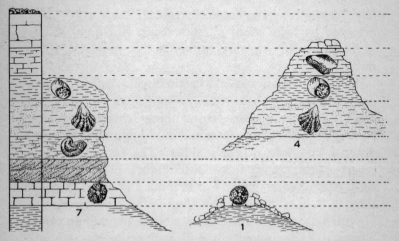

How index fossils are used to built up a geologic section, which is shown at the left without its fossils.

series can be extended until it includes deposits that are still settling and many others that accumulated during the very ancient past. The final product, as we have said, is a record of earth's history that extends through more than 3000 million years.

This record can be put into words—words that already fill many books. The tale can also be condensed into a two-page time scale. This scale divides the past into eras, ages, periods and epochs, mentions some of the things that lived during those times, and notes changes that took place on earth. Like the rocks in a geologic section, these time divisions are shown with the first (oldest) at the bottom and the last (youngest) at the top. Each division is given a name, just as we name periods and epochs of human history.

But remember: These are geologic eras and ages, not ages established in years. Fossils can tell us that one rock formation was deposited in Early Cambrian times, another during the Eocene Epoch, and so on. But no fossil can say that Cambrian rocks are 500 million years old, or Eocene beds a mere 50 million. Such figures must be determined by

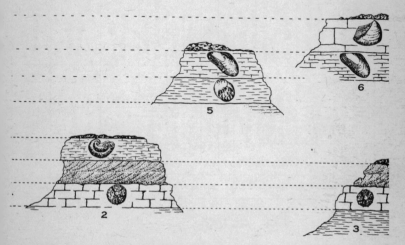

Numbers 1 to 7 show the beds in individual exposures. They are matched, or correlated, by their different fossils.

A TIME SCALE OF EARTH HISTORY

Eras	Periods and Epochs		When They Began	Changes in Lands, Seas, and Living Things
CENOZOIC or Era of Mammals	Quaternary Period	Recent Epoch	8,000 to about 10,000 years ago.	Great glaciers melted for the last time; climates grew warm. Many large land mammals died out near end of epoch. Marine animals began to live in their present homes.
		Pleistocene Epoch, also called the Great Ice Age	One million years ago (old system of division); 2.5 to 3 million years on new system.	Glaciers repeatedly spread over much of Europe, Asia, and North America. Climates and seas were cold when glaciers spread, but warm during interglacial times. Mammals grew large and varied; man evolved.
	Tertiary Period	Pliocene Epoch	13 million	High mountains, including the Rockies, formed as this period began; the Andes, Alps, Cascades, and Himalayas rose in later epochs. Seas seldom covered much of the continents. Mammals became common and varied on land; sharks and bony fish were plentiful. Modern types of corals, clams, snails, etc. became dominant in seas; ammonoids and belemnoids died out but squids and octopi became common. Land plants became more and more like those of the present day.
		Miocene Epoch	25 million	
		Oligocene Epoch	36 million	
		Eocene Epoch	58 million	
		Paleocene Epoch	63 or more million years ago	
MESOZOIC or Era of Reptiles	Cretaceous Period		135 million years ago	Lands generally were low, climates were mild, and bird-hipped dinosaurs were abundant and varied. Seas spread widely; ammonoids, belemnoids, and relatives of oysters were common, as were marine reptiles.
	Jurassic Period		180 million years ago	Lands were low; seas covered much of Europe; there were deserts, volcanoes, and swampy forests in western North America. Ammonoids, belemnoids, and marine reptiles were common; near the end of the period, lizard-hipped dinosaurs became very large and spread round the world.
	Triassic Period		230 million years ago	Seas covered much of Europe; ammonoids became common. Ichthyosaurs and early plesiosaurs evolved, as did other reptilian groups and mammals. Lizard-hipped dinosaurs became common, but most of them were small.

PALEOZOIC or Era of Ancient Life		Permian Period	280 million years ago	Coal swamps were much reduced; mountains formed in eastern North America; glaciers spread in South Africa. Large amphibians and reptiles lived in swampy lowlands; shark-like fish and early ammonoids were common.
	Carboniferous Periods	Pennsylvanian Period	330 million years ago	Coal was deposited in great swamps; seas spread but did not last long; mountain-building continued in the East and in Europe. Amphibians and reptiles became good-sized and common; crinoids grew much less abundant.
		Mississippian Period	345 to 355 million years ago	Seas covered much of North America, especially early in this period. Mountain-building in the East. Sea lilies and sea buds (crinoids and blastoids) were very abundant, but brachiopods and trilobites were less so.
		Devonian Period	405 to 410 million years ago	Most of North America was low and flat; seas spread widely though mountains began to rise and forests grew on low deltas. In the Old Red basins of Europe, fish evolved into amphibians as they tried to remain in water.
		Silurian Period	430 million years ago	Europe remained mountainous, but most of North America was low and much of it was under salt water. Marine life was abundant; jawless "fish" continued to evolve; sea scorpions were common in brackish waters.
		Ordovician Period	500 million years ago	Shifting seas covered more than half of North America, but mountains formed in the East and in Europe. Most corals remained small, but brachiopods and trilobites became common and straight cephalopods grew very large.
		Cambrian Period	570 to 620 million years ago	Most of North America was low, after mountain-building in the Great Lakes region at the end of Precambrian times. Marine animals, especially brachiopods and trilobites, became common fossils, but many other groups existed.
		PRECAMBRIAN ERAS (Variously divided on the different continents)	Probably more than 3500 million years ago	Many changes in lands and seas; mountain-building in various parts of the world; great volcanic eruptions; formations of important ore deposits; relatively few fossils.

comparing the quantities of radioactive materials that were originally contained in rocks with others into which they have disintegrated, or "decayed." Since the speed of disintegration is constant for each substance, these studies yield dates such as those used in the following chapters and in our general time scale.

"Radioactive" dates are not precise; some contain probable errors of several million years. Most dates also are not final; new determinations will change and improve them, and so will new ideas as to where dividing lines should be drawn. Qualified experts will deal with these matters—and since specimens, data, and human minds vary, a century may go by before the final figures come in.

Shall we wait? Not if we want to achieve proportion in our view of life's history. This was unnecessary a century ago, when people "knew" that the earth was created on October 22, 4004 B.C., and that all life appeared before the first weekend. Today, however, we need to express geologic time in intelligible terms. We want to tell how much longer one period was than another; how much time fish took to produce four-legged descendants, and whether Ice-age glaciers melted "when the world was young" or only a few thousand years ago. To do any of these things we must translate geologic ages into years. Since they are numbered in thousands, millions, and hundreds or thousands of millions, does it matter too much that the figures we use are averaged and rounded out, and will some day be refined?

These beds of shale near Green River, Utah, settled one upon another in a lake whose basin sank during millions of years. Index fossils show that the lake existed during the Eocene Epoch.

4   SHELLS, SEA-MUD, AND
MOUNTAINS

WE HAVE AGREED that fossils are remains or traces of things that lived during past geologic times and were buried in rocks of the earth's crust. There the ancient organisms lay until rains, rivers, rock slides, power shovels, or collectors' picks brought them to light again.

Fossils that are merely washed out of the ground soon become worthless; weather damages them as it did the "boulders" that lay around Bone Cabin. Most remains dug up by power shovels meet their fate as surely, and more rapidly, in rock crushers, cement mills, or lime kilns. Only fossils that are collected, saved, and studied with care can tell the story of life through earth's past. The length of that story astounds many people, and so does the part contributed by water-dwelling organisms that did not have backbones. Many were not even animals or plants, though they still appear under those headings in old or conservative books.

The tale told by these fossils began 1600 to 2700 million years ago. Blue-green algae have been reported from rocks of the latter age; algae, bacteria, and perhaps other creatures occur in iron-bearing beds of northern Michigan whose age has been determined as 1600 and 1800 million years. Such fossils are rare for two reasons: because they were not often preserved, and because they are so small that they are easily overlooked. Many have to be enlarged 250 to 325 times before they can be examined.

Things changed during the following ages; by 1,250,000,000 B.C. or so seas contained banks and reefs of red or blue-green algae that built stony masses while they were alive. Some of these "heads" are barely an inch in width, but others are more than 16 feet. Among later algal banks are worm burrows filled with sand, a few things that seem to be lamp-shells, and a jellyfish. Much later—just before the Cambrian Period began—other jellyfish, worms, and soft corals called sea pens left impressions in South Australian sandstones.

In our time scale, the Precambrian eras end in one simple line. That scale, however, condenses events that were long and complex, and differed on different parts of the earth. At some places sea bottoms became land; in others mountains were built and worn away; in still others sand filled embayments while glaciers covered nearby lands. Our line, in short, represents a series of events that continued through millions of years.

Fossils from Cambrian Seas

During that time several groups of animals developed hard parts that could be petrified. We say this because Early Cambrian seas were inhabited by varied animals that could not have sprung into existence as a new period began. Petrified fossils include stony sponges that built banks as much as 200 feet thick and 400 miles long and small snails that left actual shells as well as trails made while they crawled over mud devouring algae. On other muddy bottoms lived undoubted brachiopods, or lamp-shells, whose English name means nothing until we note that some later types, when divided and turned upside down, were shaped like diminutive Greek lamps. Early Cambrian species were small and thin-shelled, and many anchored themselves to sandy or muddy bottoms by means of fleshy stalks, as their relatives do today. Though brachiopod shells have two parts, or valves, the bodies differ radically from those of "bivalved" clams.

Far more active than brachiopods were creatures whose fossils are often called "petrified butterflies." Most of them were broad, thin animals 1 to 8 inches long, and they were trilobites, not butterflies. We shall examine a few outstanding Cambrian types and their successors in Chapter 5.

Two types of algal "heads," or stromatolites, from Late Precambrian rocks of Glacier National Park, Montana.

So much for Early Cambrian life as we trace it in petrified fossils. The record still is incomplete, for later formations contain organisms whose ancestors must have been evolving since Precambrian times. Besides glass sponges, lamp-shells, and trilobites, one Middle Cambrian deposit contains specialized jellyfish, as well as naked, spiny, and tube-building worms, creatures that probably were sea cucumbers, and some that looked like clams and shrimps but were related to trilobites. With these fossils, collectors also find silky seaweeds and others with broad leaflike blades which are far from being primitive.

After the Cambrian

Ever since fossils first became common, they have recorded events that are repeated over and over again. One of these is the appearance of new organisms: species, families, and larger groups that did not exist before. Some arose through step-by-step changes in well-known ancestors, but others had few if any known forebears. This was true of most Cambrian animals, which had no known relatives among Precambrian fossils.

Many important groups appeared as epochs or periods began. Then came times of expansion, during which new groups produced descendants that differed in appearance and lived in different ways. Many became amazingly well fitted, or adapted, to their surroundings and the things they had to do to live.

Adaptation was one kind of success; variety and abundance were others. Groups that were varied, abundant, and well adapted lived for millions of years, but sooner or later most of these successful creatures declined or became extinct. Either could happen at almost any time, but extinctions were most widespread at the end of epochs or periods, when seas shifted, lands rose or sank, and climates changed greatly. Highly adapted creatures were often the first to die out. Unspecialized forms might linger on or even produce descendants that evolved into different groups.

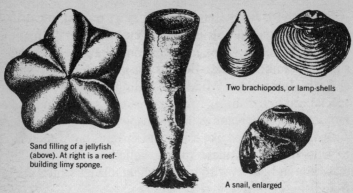

Sand filling of a jellyfish
(above). At right is a reef-
building limy sponge.

Two brachiopods, or lamp-shells

A snail, enlarged

Some Early Cambrian fossils

Now and then, however, unspecialized creatures neither
died out nor evolved into new ones. They lived on and on
instead, surviving through epochs, periods, and even eras
without important change. Those that exist today appear to
be so antique that we often call them living fossils.

Two of these events—decline and extinction—took place at
the end of Cambrian times. Hordes of established trilobites
and brachiopods died out as broad, shallow seas became land.
When the Ordovician Period began and new seas spread,
they brought hordes of creatures that were characterized by
thick, even stony, shells and supports.

No one knows why these structures were developed, for
Ordovician seas did not differ much from those of the
Cambrian Period. Yet some corals built separate horn-
shaped supports for their bodies while others lived in stony
colonies. Bryozoans, whose name deceptively means "moss
animals," also built colonies that grew to be large and ornate
in Late Ordovician seas. Brachiopods became abundant and
many kinds developed shells that grew to be very thick or
were strengthened by prominent ridges. Snail shells were
round, pointed, or flat on one side and deeply convex on the
other.

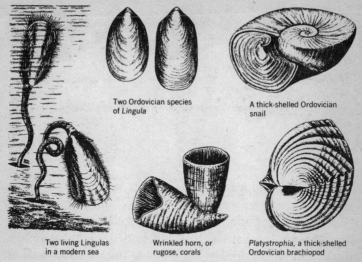

Two Ordovician species
of *Lingula*

A thick-shelled Ordovician
snail

Two living Lingulas
in a modern sea

Wrinkled horn, or
rugose, corals

Platystrophia, a thick-shelled
Ordovician brachiopod

Some typical Ordovician fossils and two modern Lingulas

Middle Ordovician seas also sheltered brachiopods whose descendants are the most successful of living fossils. Called *Lingula* (little tongue), they were and still are small, thin-shelled creatures that pushed tough stalks into mud or sand under shallow sea water. While the animals fed, their stalks were extended; when they were disturbed, their stalks contracted and pulled them into the sediment. *Lingula* was most plentiful on shallow, sandy sea bottoms like those on which it lives today. Among the Philippine Islands, these brachiopods are so abundant that storm waves pile them up to heights of 12 to 30 inches along miles of beach. Yet the creatures reproduce in such abundance that their numbers are not permanently diminished. Instead, destruction seems to give new individuals a chance to grow.

Many Ordovician sea-dwellers died out, but the next two periods saw a great increase in shells and supports. Corals built "horns" that were 25 inches long and 3 inches thick; clams developed sturdy shells; starfish protected themselves

A complete lamp-shell   One part, or valve   An ancient lamp

Why brachiopods are often called lamp-shells

with plates of the material that makes up limestone. Even one-celled creatures nicknamed "forams" built small, coiled shells which supported and, when necessary, covered their jellylike flesh. Similar shells would settle by trillions on the bottom of a Mississippian sea, forming thick beds of buff or whitish rock. Known commercially as Indiana Limestone, it is often used in the walls of large buildings.

Thick shells, plates, and supports resisted destruction, and therefore had a chance to become fossils. But why are those fossils often so abundant that hundreds or thousands may be collected in an afternoon? Why are many unbroken or even unworn? Finally, why are they now on land although they lived and died in seas?

Our answer to the first question depends on the fact that these fossils lived in shallow seas which spread over regions that were parts of continents, not oceans. In this they resembled the present-day Baltic Sea, North Sea, and Hudson Bay, which now cover 860,000 square miles of Europe and North America to depths that average 180, 308, and 420 feet. In North America alone, Ordovician seas covered more than 5 million square miles.

Since ancient seas were shallow, they were well lighted, and extensive areas were not very far from shore. This meant that they received minerals from land—and minerals plus sunlight are the basis of abundant sea life. Today it begins with tiny plants that make the water dull green; they are eaten by small animals, and so on up to giant sharks and whales. Similar food chains must have existed in ancient times, though large sharks and whales did not exist before the Cenozoic Era. With whales or without them, however, hordes of fossils exist because ancient seas were good places to live in and provided plentyof food.

Seas that were good to live in also favoured preservation of shells and other hard parts without much wear or breakage. It is true that some ancient waters were stormy, with waves that rolled corals over and over and ground shells into bits. In other seas, dead creatures were carried in currents, but so gently that many shells were not deeply worn or broken, and jointed animals were not torn apart. Some seas, finally, were so quiet that mud sank to the bottom and buried its inhabitants where they had lived and died. This is shown by bryozoans and corals whose remains still stand upright in shale, and by others that spread in delicate networks over what once was clay. Some fine-grained sandstones contain brachiopods which are crowded together with their tips, or beaks, directed downward and the openings of their shells upward. These plainly are beds or "banks" of fossils which still occupy both the places and positions in which they spent their lives.

From Sea Bottoms to Land

Because many fossils lived, died, and were buried under shallow water, we are tempted to think that a slight shift would raise the beds that contain them and so turn sea bottoms into land. Slight shifts, however, could not put most marine deposits where they are today. As a rule, these rocks accumulated on sea bottoms that sank throughout epochs or periods, and often sank again after new periods began. As a result, beds settled one on top of another in series that became hundreds or thousands of feet thick. Some of these series still lie under salt water. Others come to the surface in mountain ranges and hills or lie beneath rolling land and plains. Deep wells have been bored through 2 to almost 8 miles of strata under western plains.

These rocks have plainly been pushed upward, since they settled under seas. The task required vast amounts of energy, but it did not always take the form of earth-shaking, catastrophic upheavals. Throughout much of North America, marine formations were raised 500 to 5000 feet above sea level so gently and so uniformly that many show neither bending nor breaking. Others slope no more steeply than well-engineered roads.

Such rocks also appear in high plateau like the one that rises both north and south of Arizona's famous Grand Canyon. They are uncommon in mountains, however, for most strata that make up peaks have been pushed slantwise, broken into long blocks, or tilted so much that they dip steeply or appear to stand on edge. Other beds were squeezed until they arched into folds that would now be 2 to 5 miles high if their crests had not been worn away. In some places, compression became so great that it broke mountain ranges 80 to 700 miles long and pushed them obliquely upward for distances of 10 to 30 miles.

Where uplift has been greatest, it has brought rocks from depths of several thousand feet and has left them in mountains. The tip of Everest, now 29,028 feet high, consists of sandy marine limestones that were once covered by later beds.

Few of us can collect on Mount Everest, but it is not hard to find places where fossil-bearing rocks have been raised a mile or more. East of the Silver Gate to Yellowstone Park, for example, U.S. Highway 212 passes Beartooth Lake at an altitude of 8912 feet, and he who climbs Beartooth Butte may find fossils of Cambrian, Ordovician, and Devonian ages. West of Los Alamos, New Mexico, State Highway 4 crosses slopes of marine Mississippian limestone from which brachiopods have been weathered. In Glacier National Park,

Montana, a paved highway crosses Logan Pass at 6664 feet, and the parking space at the summit is rimmed by beds of marine Precambrian algae. Other algae are found in a mountain from whose top at least two miles of strata have been removed by erosion. When we raise our binoculars to scan those cliffs, we are likely to see a mountain goat and her kid, climbing to the ledge where they will rest until late afternoon. Though those goats are alpine animals, their resting place is far below the ledge that contains the second algal deposit.

Do we need better evidence that this particular sea bottom has been pushed to a height of more than 3 miles above the depths at which it once lay?

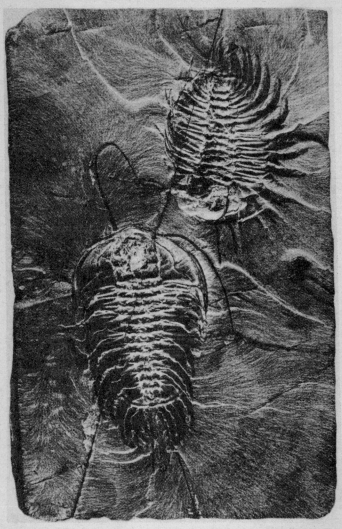

Two Middle Cambrian trilobites, *Olenoides*, from British Columbia. This specimen is in the United States National Museum.

5   SKIN-CRUSTED
TRILOBITES

TRILOBITES, AS we know, are sometimes called petrified butterflies; compact species have also been mistaken for stony nuts and toads. Actually, these fossils belong to a class in the phylum of animals with jointed feet, which also includes crabs, lobsters, insects, centipedes and spiders.

The name trilobite means "three-lobed creature." We readily see that the trilobite body contains three parts which look like head, abdomen, and tail, but the lobes that account for the name run lengthwise and are separated by grooves. Unusually well-preserved fossils also show feelers, or antennae, as well as legs, and eyes that contain many sections, or facets.

Though trilobites were not simple, they were the first animals to leave large numbers of fossils. In many Early Cambrian formations, trilobites are the only fossils that are common and very well preserved.

There are three reasons for this. First, trilobites really were common in many places and at many times. Second, trilobite shells were made of material that was not easily destroyed. Third, the animals shed their shells as they grew and developed new ones, as crabs do today. The number of shells probably varied, but several kinds produced a dozen before they became full-grown. One of these animals might leave a dozen fossils, each showing the entire body at one stage of its development. When shells were broken to pieces, the number of fossils increased with every piece.

Though we usually say that trilobites had shells, *skin-crusts* is a better term. A shell is almost any hard covering: a nut shell, turtle shell, clam shell, and so on. But a nut shell is woody, a turtle shell is bone, and a clam shell consists of hard, limy material. Many trilobite shells became hard, but they always began as flexible coats that were built on the

An Early Cambrian trilobite, *Olenellus*, shedding its skin-crust, which broke open on the cephalon, or "head." The cast-off crust was tough and durable, and readily became a fossil.

surface of the skin. Throughout life they remained thin and flexible where they covered movable joints, and the skin readily separated from them when the animals prepared to shed. As its skin-crust split, each trilobite wriggled out and probably hid until its skin was able to build a new and larger crust.

Changes in Trilobites

No one knows when or how trilobites evolved; they apparently did so before skin-crusts grew thick enough to be petrified. One theory says the group began with little, eyeless animals whose descendants added sections as well as organs to their bodies. A widely held theory, which we shall follow, derives trilobites from jointed sea worms whose bodies contained many sections, or segments, each bearing one pair of legs. As ages passed the segments (also called somites) widened; those that lay just behind the head combined with it and so built up the cephalon, which included both head and forward part of the body. At the rear, other segments combined to form the pygidium, which was much more than a tail. Between these two divisions of the body lay the thorax, which still consisted of segments linked by movable joints, with legs on the underside of each section. Portions of the cephalon and pygidium also retained their legs, though these are seldom preserved in fossils.

Still following this theory, we select five trilobites to show the results of these evolutionary changes (p.46). Specimens 1 and 2 are Early Cambrian types called *Olenellus*; the former may closely resemble the creature that first became a trilobite. The pygidium seems to be the original button-shaped end of the body, and the thorax, with its twenty-six sections, suggests a broad, many-jointed worm. The fifteenth segment, however, bears a long spine, and the cephalon has become complex. Its central lobe shows traces of five segments behind the original head.

In one respect Specimen 2 is still more primitive, for its thorax contains forty-four segments instead of twenty-six. But the last twenty-nine segments seem to have shrunk, though the first fourteen have widened and nine of them end in spines. The cephalon also is wide, though only three segments appear behind the original head. If there are more, the grooves that once divided them have vanished.

Specimen 5, the Middle Cambrian *Ogygopsis*, is a combination of contrasts. The whole animal is flattened and broad, its width being two thirds of its length. The thorax contains only eight blunt segments, but five and the head may be traced in the cephalon and at least fourteen appear in the broad pygidium. There is no trace of the long spine seen in *Olenellus*.

These are substantial changes, but they seem trifling when we compare them with others which—if our theory is correct--are shown by Specimens 3 and 4. Though they are fully grown, both fossils measure less than three eighths of an inch in length. Number 3 has three thoracic segments and traces of eight in the pygidium; in 4 the number are two and three. In contrast to our first *Olenellus*, this trilobite has lost at least twenty-three segments or has combined them into its pygidium and cephalon. Like Number 3, it also has lost its eyes. As a result, we cannot always tell which end of the little creature is which.

Changes such as these took place again and again in various combinations, for trilobites were a complex class whose members evolved independently through some 390 million years. Long after our fourth fossil had lost most of its segments, one trilobite still possessed eighteen thoracic segments and a two-part pygidium. Several Ordovician and Silurian forms had pygidia that bore no hint of segments—but in Permian times, when trilobites were dying out, one called *Ameura* carried clear traces of eighteen pygidial segments. In one Pennsylvanian species they numbered twenty-six!

Trilobites differed as much in shape, ornamentation, and size as they did in the number of their parts. *Bumastus*, for example, was deep-bodied and smooth, with rounded cephalon and pygidium. Several genera were broad and flattened, with their segments so nearly separate that they suggest clusters of leaves. Other trilobites were small, blunt, and compact, with thick, rough shells, but some tapered to

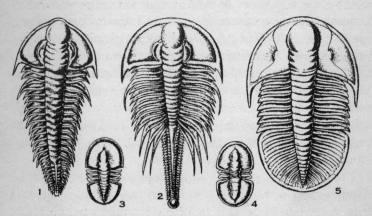

Evolutionary changes in trilobites. Number 1 is a primitive Early Cambrian species of *Olenellus*; 2 is more advanced but still has many sections behind its long spine. Number 5 is a Middle Cambrian species of another genus; it shows that at least fourteen segments have been combined in its pygidium. Numbers 3 and 4 are regarded as highly evolved Middle Cambrian trilobites that have lost most of their segments as well as their eyes.

both ends or developed long spines that projected from both cephalon and pygidium. When the thorax also became spiny, the creatures must have resembled animated burrs.

Many spiny trilobites were small, but one was 28 inches long and another, called *Tertaspis*, measured 18 to 20 inches. Its crust was dotted with prickers and spikes; its cephalon ended in long spines, as did the segments of its thorax and those that had been combined into the pygidium. Since large spines were set with small ones, the skin-crust provided a prickly mouthful for any creature that attacked *Tertaspis*.

How Did They Live?

Trilobites apparently were descended from jointed worms, and many kinds combined wormlike ways with others appropriate to the animals' new status. Primitive types skimmed over the sea bottom by means of their legs, but in swimming the many-jointed bodies also undulated. When crawling became desirable, all trilobites relied on their legs, which often dug into soft mud as they carried their owners forward. Crescent-shaped eyes looked forward, sideways, upward and a little to the rear, but eyes on stalks were still more versatile. Antennae smelled or tasted food, which often consisted of burrowing worms. *Olenellus* apparently used legs on the underside of the cephalon to dig out worms and push them into the mouth. In spring, female trilobites dug pits and laid eggs in them. Sand then filled the pits and protected the eggs until they hatched and the young ones swam away.

This account is inferential; no human being ever saw a trilobite swim, crawl, dig for food, or excavate a nest for its eggs. But we do know how a trilobite's jointed legs and body could move, fossil trails are fairly common, and irregular pits are just what we should find where the animals dug food from mud or loose sand. Other pits are more regular in form, and their sides bear marks that correspond to the legs and spines of trilobites found in the same strata. These pits also

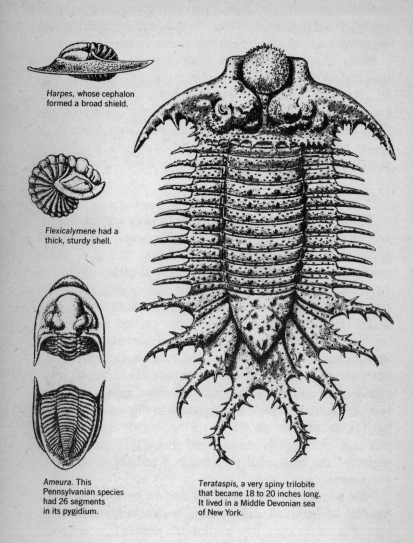

Harpes, whose cephalon formed a broad shield.

Flexicalymene had a thick, sturdy shell.

Ameura. This Pennsylvanian species had 26 segments in its pygidium.

Terataspis, a very spiny trilobite that became 18 to 20 inches long. It lived in a Middle Devonian sea of New York.

Enrolled and spiny trilobites

resemble those dug in loose sand by modern horseshoe crabs, which eat worms and are the nearest living relatives of trilobites.

Egg-laying in pits rests on similar evidence. Some hardened fillings are deeper and more precise than those that seem to have been dug for food; markings closely match the spines and cephalons of *Olenellus*. Alternations of mudstone and sand indicate that these pits were dug in the spring, which is the season when horseshoe crabs dig pits for their eggs. May we not infer that trilobites shared, if they did not invent, this instinct?

The thick, bulbous body of *Bumastus* was poorly adapted to swimming or crawling. This trilobite probably ploughed through mud, eating worms as it went. Since the eyes were

How some trilobites lived. Number 1, *Paradoxides* swimming. Number 2, *Isotelus* lying on the sea bottom with its pygidium thrust into mud. Number 3, *Cryptolithus*, an eyeless creature that crept on mud. Number 4, *Thaleops* enrolled; arrows point to the eyes, which were on stalks. Number 5, *Bumastus* ploughing through mud in search of food. These creatures actually lived at different times.

high up on the cephalon, the stirred-up sediment did not blind them.

Getting mud on one's eye was no problem for trilobites that had lost their eyes as well as most of their body segments. These creatures probably lay or crept slowly on muddy sea bottoms, eating both dead material and little animals that lived in it.

We need not guess at the habits of trilobites with smooth, flattened skin-crusts, pygidia shaped like trenching tools, and eyes on stalks or on top of the cephalon. Fossils sometimes lie just where they lived, with pygidia thrust down into what was a sea bottom and the rest of the body lying upon it. In this position, the animals could eat food that drifted over the mud, but could not be carried away by currents.

Skin-crusts into Armour

We sometimes say that trilobites were supreme in Early Paleozoic seas. That doubtless was true at some times and places; the largest Cambrian animal was a trilobite 18 inches long that weighed about 8 pounds, and a late Ordovician species 30 inches in length was bigger than any of its neighbours. But all trilobites were mild-mannered eaters of plants, carrion, and worms, and they neither fought nor carried weapons. When predators appeared they could only use their skin-crusts as armour.

Terataspis was doubly protected, for his thick, hard crust resisted attack and his spines discouraged efforts to turn him over. Smooth-shelled *Dipleura* folded his shieldlike cephalon against his pygidium and was completely covered; *Calymene* and its relatives built thick skin-crusts that were strengthened by ridges. When these trilobites rolled up tightly they presented surfaces that were difficult to break.

Several trilobites had cephalons that seem much too large for their small bodies. Some crept on sandy bottoms, but others pushed forward with the broad rim of the cephalon just below the surface of loose mud. None of these creatures could roll very tightly, but all were able to tuck the thorax and pygidium under the expanded "head."

Enemies and Extinction

What predators called forth these defences? Those of Cambrian times have not been discovered, though a few petrified trilobites show that sections had been bitten from their thoraxes. In Chapter 6, however, we shall see that the Ordovician Period brought a host of molluscs with muscular arms and sharp beaks. Ranging from a few inches to 10 or 12 feet in length, these creatures preyed on anything big enough to be worth eating. Though trilobites were less meaty than present-day crabs and lobsters, the new predators found them to be desirable food.

As ages passed, these hungry molluscs were joined by predatory fish. As enemies increased, trilobites such as *Terataspis* covered themselves with spines while types with smooth, thin skin-crusts died out. Then, in Late Devonian times, the whole class entered a long decline that ended in extinction as the Permian Period closed. The last survivors were small animals whose thick armour was strengthened by swellings and ridges. Many of the latter still represented segments that had become part of cephalon and pygidium millions of years before.

6   THE REPETITIVE
HORN-SHELLS

SILURIAN SEA WEEDS swayed as a creature in a coiled shell darted past them. It swam shell-first, with its body and soft, fleshy arms behind, driving itself by jets of water that came from a tube under its head. When the jets stopped, the shell sank beside a trilobite and the arms reached out to seize it.

The trilobite was a half-grown *Bumastus*, plowing its way through mud. As it struggled to dig more deeply, the attacker came part-way out of his shell. His body was smooth, but a hood of rough skin spread above his big eyes. They and the arms made the creature resemble a cuttlefish, squid, or octopus that had backed into the shell of a tightly rolled snail.

The resemblance was natural, for the Silurian predator was related to all these animals. It was also connected, much more closely, with the pearly (or chambered) nautilus. All five are—or were—molluscs belonging to the class of cephalopods. They were given this name, which means "head-foot," because their bodies are so tightly folded that the head and foot are together.

Cephalopods are divided into three subclasses, but only two are characterized by shells large enough to cover the entire body. One of these subclasses is made up of ammonoids, which have been extinct since the end of the Cretaceous Period. The outer shell-covered subclass, called nautiloids, includes all cephalopods whose shells are built like the shell of the modern nautilus. Since many members of both subclasses have names that end in *ceras*, which is Greek for "horn," we may give them the English name of horn-shells.

Weatherworn fossils or a modern shell that has been cut in half shows the essential characteristics of nautiloids. The shell is always divided into parts, or chambers, by curved partitions called septa which were built by the rear end of the body. The last chamber is the longest and largest; it also contained the body when the horn-shell was alive. A fleshy stalk extended backward through the septa and covered itself with a tube of shelly material. This tube (the siphuncle) is thin in some shells but is thick in others. Thick siphuncles often look like backbones or chains of hollow beads.

Changes in Horn-shells

The horn-shell that caught *Bumastus* was a nautiloid that lived in a sea which covered northern Illinois about 420 million years ago. In spite of its great age, the creature was neither the first member of its subclass nor a primitive one. Nautiloids appeared in Early Cambrian seas, as tiny creatures with straight, cone-shaped shells less than a quarter inch long. As time passed, their descendants grew larger and larger, until some straight horn-shells were 8, 10 or even 12 feet in length. These giants lived in Middle Ordovician seas that extended from New York to Alabama, Kansas, and Saskatchewan.

The living nautilus helps us determine what fossil horn-shells looked like. We already know that the body was short; the round eyes were covered with skin and had slits instead of pupils. The arms could stretch out and pull, but they had no suckers like those on the arms of an octopus. The mouth, which was hidden among the arms, had a beak like a parrot's turned upside down. With that beak, the Silurian hunter bit chunks from the trilobite it had captured.

Some petrified horn-shells preserve stripes and zigzag bands of colour which grade from dark above to light below. The animals probably lay on the sea bottom much of the time, or crawled about slowly by means of their arms. When they had to move rapidly, they swam.

Some Middle Silurian horn-shells. Number 1 is the species that captured *Bumastus*; 2 is a straight-shelled relative; 3 is an empty, broken shell. It shows part of the living chamber, ten septa, and the siphuncle, as well as nine empty chambers.

Old restorations sometimes showed long, straight horn-shells darting to and fro like underwater missiles. Those pictures, however, overlooked the shells, and they were too big to be ignored. If a shell had been empty except for the stalk of flesh, it would have risen until the animal hung head downward, with only its arms touching the bottom. If it had tried to swim, it would have shot to the surface. Had it attempted to turn, it would have bobbed this way and that, but still would have risen to the surface.

These things would have happened *if*, and they probably *did* happen during Cambrian times. But as straight nautiloids progressed they made changes that kept their shells under control. The simplest change was made again and again, as one nautiloid after another added weight, or ballast, to its shell. Some kinds deposited material around the siphuncle; others thickened the septa, and still others did both. Shells sometimes became so heavy that we wonder whether the creatures could swim. Perhaps they spent most of their time lying on the sea bottom.

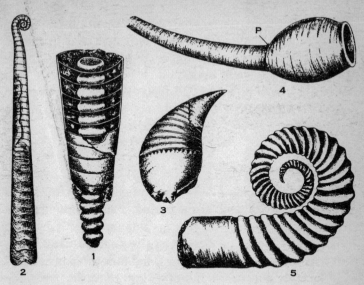

How nautiloids changed. Number 1, part of a cone-shaped species
with thin septa and a thick "beaded" siphuncle. Number 2, *Lituites*,
which coiled and then became straight; it probably lived in this
position. Number 3, a short, curved shell with a large living
chamber. Number 4, a slender shell that suddenly became swollen.
It soon broke off a P. Number 5, a wrinkled, loosely coiled shell that
became smooth and straight during old age.

Even empty shells would not become unwieldy if they
were short. When we make something too long we cut or
break off a portion, and some horn-shells developed a similar
method. For much of their lives, they built slender shells that
were gently curved instead of straight. Then the animals
suddenly became larger than they had been, and began to
build swollen shells. Just behind each new part was a line of
weakness, and there the empty shell broke off.

This was a roundabout method; why not just build a short
shell? Though no cephalopod was bright enough to ask that
question, many kinds evolved answers to it. Some did so by
building very short, wide shells that were straight or gently
curved. Then, when the animals were almost ready to stop

growing, they narrowed the apertures of their living chambers until they were mere slits or irregular openings. Instead of crawling or swimming, these creatures probably drifted with their shells upright, their bodies downward, and their arms reaching out to find food. The openings were so narrow, however, that they could not pull large victims to their mouths.

Curves and Coils

Early Cambrian nautiloids were straight, but curved shells appeared before the end of the period. There were others in Ordovician and later seas, for curvature apparently evolved several times. Some of these fossils were relatives of shells with narrow or irregular openings, and they probably floated with the body downward. But other curved fossils have wide openings and zigzag colour markings that are dark all the way round. These creatures must have kept most of the body outside the shell, using their arms to crawl on one flattened side. They had evolved a new substitute for the flat foot which their ancestors had lost when they became cephalopods.

Tightly coiled horn-shells appeared in Early Ordovician seas, and so did others whose coils were open. Both got long shells into little space. Since the coils were not heavily weighted, they helped keep the animals right-side-up and were not in the way when they swam. Coiled nautiloids survived long after straight ones died out, for the living nautilus is coiled.

Although coiled shells were useful, some nautiloids soon began to uncoil. But they did not merely straighten out, as we straighten a length of hose. Instead, they began by building tightly coiled shells—many, in fact, kept on doing so until they were half or two thirds grown. Some kinds then opened up in loose whorls or abruptly changed to straight living chambers that lost the ridges and frills of earlier stages. Only

Three contrasting nautiloids. Number 1 had a short shell with a narrow, irregular opening. Number 2, a curved shell whose owner crawled on one flattened side of the body, like a snail. Number 3, a species that coiled like a snail but seldom crawled, since its body was small. The colour markings on 1 and 2 show plainly in fossils.

a few, such as *Lituites*, built small coils and followed them with straight, compressed shells that were eight to twelve times longer than the diameters of their coils. Millions of years later, however, other nautiloids coiled in low spires resembling those that had long since been developed by several groups of snails.

Relatives of "Ammon's Stone"

We have traced three types of repetition among ancient cephalopods. In one, nautiloids of several different groups evolved curved shells from straight ones. In the second, other groups of shells straightened after building coils, and in the third, shells that had formed flat coils duplicated the spires of many snails. Another subclass, however, went still further. Besides repeating the shell forms already developed by nautiloids, they evolved some variants of their own whose repetitions involved the septa, not the shape of the shell.

These new horn-shells were the ammonoids, or relatives of *Ammonites*. That mollusc, whose name means "Ammon's stone," supposedly resembled sheep's horns worn by Ammon, foremost of ancient Egyptian gods. Ammonoid

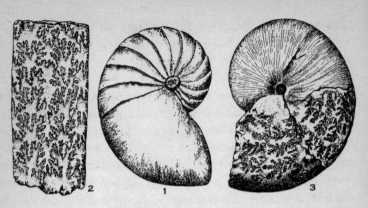

How nautiloids differ from ammonoids. Number 1 is the hardened filling of a nautiloid, showing gently curved sutures. Number 2, straight portion of *Baculites*, with elaborately crumpled septa and sutures. Number 3, a coiled ammonoid with equally elaborate sutures.

bodies were deeply wrinkled behind and therefore built bent or crumpled septa instead of partitions that curved smoothly like those of nautiloids. This did not affect the outer surface, but it produced zigzag or very ornate sutures where septa joined the inside of the shell. In their most elaborate forms, these sutures suggest lace or the complex leaflets of ferns.

Ammonoids appeared in Middle Devonian seas, when they resembled narrow nautiloids. Long before the Paleozoic Era ended, however, some descendants of Devonian species built narrow shells with ridges or keels, around their edges. Other types became small and almost ball-shaped or built squat shells with low, broad openings through which the body and arms could extend. Some bizarre creatures coiled in crude triangles or built triangles for a while and then finished their lives in bulb-shaped chambers. The sutures of these odd shells went back to gentle, almost nautiloid curves.

Ammonoids first achieved abundance in Triassic seas. Fossils of that age include shells of most types we have mentioned, as well as others with knobs and curved ridges and a few that coiled in taller spires than those of snail-shaped nautiloids. Sutures, as a rule, were more deeply crumpled than those of earlier times.

Most Triassic ammonoids died out as that period came to an end. A few types survived, however, and their descendants became both abundant and varied during Jurassic and Cretaceous times. With a few exceptions, they duplicated Triassic and earlier shapes, from balls to horns and smooth, compressed shells that reached 3 feet in diameter. Some also developed spiral coils that were higher and much more slender than any of Triassic age.

We have seen that nautiloids uncoiled at various times and in varied ways. Some Jurassic ammonoids did so, too, but Cretaceous species went further and were more bizarre. One extreme was reached by *Helicoceras*, which ranged through seas that extended from Tennessee to South Dakota, Wyoming, and Texas. *Helicoceras* coiled, opened and grew in a curve that swung sideways, turned and curved again, built a spire, and uncoiled once more. *Baculites*, however, repeated the course taken by *Lituites* during the Ordovician Period; both coiled for a while and then built slender, straight shells. Since *Baculites* was not weighted, it probably crawled or drifted at a slant, with its coil upward and its arms on the sea bottom, where they could seize food.

Scaphites and its close relatives had shells that were strengthened by ridges and bumps. Broken specimens often show only coils; complete fossils prove that the shells uncoiled or curved in reverse and then bent so abruptly that the arms must have reached the coils.

To us, such changes in shape seem confusing and wasteful; one theory says they used up so much energy that these ammonoids became extinct. Actually, both *Baculites* and *Scaphites* must have been successful, for they ranged widely and were abundant during the latter half of the Cretaceous Period. When they died out, coiled ammonoids also became extinct. If wasted energy killed *Baculites* and *Scaphites*, what brought extinction to other groups that did not uncoil?

Today, both *Baculites* and *Scaphites* are common fossils. Many specimens still preserve their pearly lustre; though most shells of *Baculites* are broken, those of *Scaphites* are often complete. Sutures of *Baculites* are so elaborate that chamber fillings interlock and do not fall apart, even when both shell and septa weather away. Such fossils are often mistaken for petrified backbones or snakes.

Baculites had ornate, interlocking sutures, as did many other ammonoids of Jurassic and Cretaceous seas. As Late Cretaceous times began, however, many ammonoids developed septa and sutures which were no more crumpled than those of typical Permian species. Though some shells were curved, more were as tightly coiled as shells whose

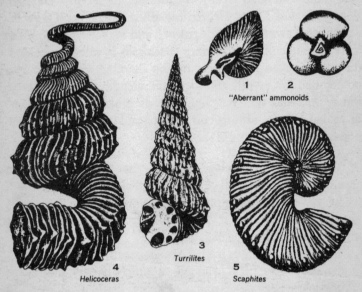

Varied ammonoids. 1 and 2 are coiled in unusual shapes; 3 resembles screw snails; 4 assumes a variety of forms at different stages; 5 is a *Scaphites* that coiled, uncoiled, and bent but died before coiling again.

sutures were more ornate than those of *Baculites*. Simplification of septa and sutures did not demand simplification of shells.

Belemnoids and Squids

We have completed our story of horn-shells, but one tale of repetition is still to be told. It begins with belemnoids, whose fossils usually resemble an old-fashioned wooden pen holder with a deep pit at the large end. The pit once held a small conical shell containing several septa and chambers.

This chambered shell tells us that belemnoids were descended from small, straight nautiloids. As we learned in Chapter 2, however, the living belemnoid was a torpedo-shaped animal whose body completely covered its hard parts. It had large round eyes, balancing fins that spread sideways, and ten fleshy arms. Two of the arms seem to have borne sucking discs that probably caught fish; the other eight arms carried paired rows of hooks that clung to soft or slippery victims.

The rocks in which fossil belemnoids are found show that the animals swam in shallow, near-shore waters as well as in

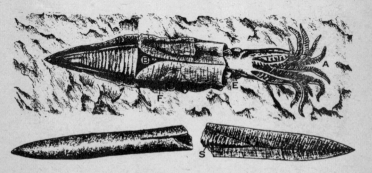

A fossil belemonoid showing eyes (E), arms (A), ink bag (B), and parts of the fins (F). Below this fossil are two guards. One, which is split lengthwise, shows part of the conical shell (S).

open seas. The creatures appeared during Mississippian times, reached their greatest abundance during the Cretaceous Period, and died out in the Eocene Epoch. Their role as active molluscan hunters was taken over by squids.

Squids may be descendants of early belemnoids; if so, they have lost all except a trace of their ancestors' shell and "pen." In spite of this, most species are torpedo-shaped swimmers with goggle eyes, balancing fins, and ten arms. In short, though they have changed so much that their ancestry is doubtful, squids resemble belemnoids in shape, speed, method of swimming and catching food, and the habit of swimming in "schools" that often range far from shore. Like belemnoids, squids defend themselves by ejecting inky liquid that paralyses pursuers' smelling organs. Predaceous fish that have been "shot" by this liquid do not recognize squids even when they touch the molluscs.

7 STALKS AND STARS

BURLINGTON, IOWA, began as a trading post on the Mississippi River. Today the city spreads over nearby hills, and its factories turn out products that range from steam turbines to electronic equipment. To fossil hunters, however, Burlington's hills are famous for the crinoids that were collected from them during the late 1800s.

Here we encounter a note which, for today's collector, becomes a discouraging refrain. Most of those crinoids were found between 1860 and 1890; fine corals were abundant beside the Ohio River during the 1870s and 80s; trilobites were scattered over a Cincinnati hillside 80 years ago but are not to be picked up today. Why are they no longer available? Why do collecting localities, like their fossils, often belong to the past?

There are many answers to these questions, but they boil down to three. The first reminds us that fossils often occur in "pockets" which formed where the organisms grew or where their remains were left by streams, waves, or currents in the sea. A small crinoid bank is such a pocket; so is the shale containing carbonized Middle Cambrian fossils, some of which are illustrated in Chapter 2. If a pocket is small it can be "worked out"; once its fossils have been collected, no more are to be found.

Our next answer is the second half of an apparent contradiction. Rain and frost, as we know, can destroy fossils; they turn corals into pebbles, break shells to bits, and reduce massive bones to boulders like those Walter Granger found at Bone Cabin. On the other hand, many invertebrates must be weathered out of rock before they can be seen, collected, and studied. Weathering is rapid in clays and soft shales, from which new supplies of fossils may appear every spring or after heavy rains. Hard limestone, however, crumbles very slowly; the crinoids collected at Burlington between 1860 and 1890 had been freed by a hundred centuries of crumbling and wear. Good collecting ended when those fossils were removed. Ten thousand years from now, specimens may become plentiful again. Meanwhile, fossil hunters who want good crinoids have to look elsewhere for them.

Finally, the spread of cities has destroyed many collecting localities, and others have succumbed to technologic changes. In Cincinnati, university buildings cover a hill where collectors once went every spring to hunt tightly rolled trilobites. The banks of Big Creek, near Cleveland, once were a source of fossil fish; during the 1920s Big Creek Basin was taken over by suburban streets, houses, and lawns. Limestone hills of Burlington have also been covered by the city that once was a trading post.

Many clay pits and quarries still operate as actively as they did long ago. But mechanical diggers do not stop to let workmen pick up fossils, and rock crushers destroy crinoids or corals as readily as they break up limestone. On the other hand, German quarries where workmen once found jellyfish, horseshoe crabs, insects, and even reptiles now stand idle

Limestone made up largely of broken crinoid stalks (left), and a cystoid with stalk and two arms (right). The limestone was found at Burlington, Iowa.

because coated metal plates do work that once required slabs of pure and evenly bedded limestone. The year-in-year-out demand for fossils is not great enough to keep quarries in operation.

Still, civilization is not wholly bad for the collector. Paved roads reach localities once inaccessible, and Jeeps go where wheel-tracks stop. Road cuts often expose fossil-bearing strata, and drills that sink oil wells bring specimens—always small ones—from rocks hundreds or thousands of feet below the surface. Acids and other chemicals are used to remove delicate specimens from rock, and X-ray machines photograph fossils while they are still covered by stone. For fossils such as crinoids, however, nothing quite equals a specimen that is weathered out of limestone, with only small bits of rock still to be removed.

Animals on Stalks

Crinoids are often called sea lilies because their cuplike or lily-shaped bodies are usually borne upon stalks. There the resemblance ends, however, for lilies are plants that live on land and crinoids are marine animals related to sea urchins and starfish. All belong to the phylum of echinoderms: animals characterized by hard plates and spines that form *in* the skin but never *upon* it, like a trilobite's crust or a nautiloid's shell. The plates and spines also consist of calcite, which is the principal mineral in limestone. As much as 85 per cent of the limestone at Burlington consists of crinoids themselves and of calcite from their plates and spines.

Echinoderms are often divided into two great groups: those with stalks and those without them. The former, however, began as small creatures shaped like eggs or flattened balls which fastened themselves directly to dead shells or lay upon hard-packed mud. Plates in the skin were many and small, and the mouth opened on the upper surface of the body. A less attractive and imposing ancestor can hardly be imagined.

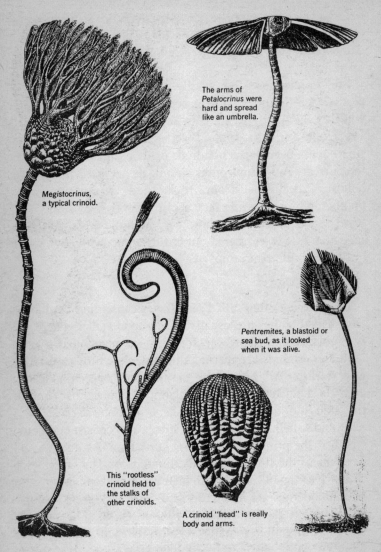

The arms of
Petalocrinus were
hard and spread
like an umbrella.

Megistocrinus,
a typical crinoid.

Pentremites, a blastoid or
sea bud, as it looked
when it was alive.

This "rootless"
crinoid held to
the stalks of
other crinoids.

A crinoid "head" is really
body and arms.

Four varied crinoids and a blastoid, or sea bud

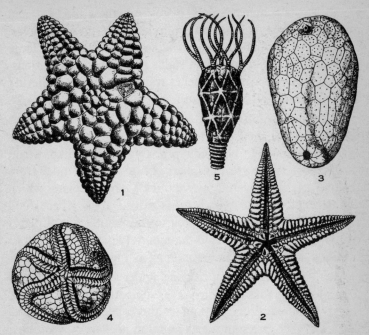

Primitive and advanced echinoderms. Number 1, *Hudsonaster*, an Ordovician starfish. Number 2, undersurface of *Devonaster*, showing opening for the mouth and the grooves that contained tube feet. Number 3, a primitive Ordovician cystoid. Number 4, an edrioaster that was attached to a shell. Number 5, a "dawn crinoid" of Cambrian age.

Ancestors need not be imposing, however; what they require is the ability to survive through thousands or millions of years plus a tendency to produce changed offspring that can live, reproduce, and repeat that process. In these respects the simple echinoderms excelled, for their direct descendants included eleven of the twelve echinoderm classes, some with stalks and others without. Three of the stalked groups became so abundant that they demand our attention here.

This statement must be qualified; some cystoids remained

stemless, had many small plates on their bodies, and probably looked like the first "spiny skins." Others, however, developed cup-shaped bodies that were covered with large plates and were supported on stalks made of round sections. Jointed arms with small branches waved to and fro, gathering food and sending it to the mouth.

Blastoids are often called petrified nuts; since their technical name means "budlike," the term "sea buds" is a substitute. In life, blastoids probably looked like small, shaggy flowers, for great numbers of tiny arms extended from the body. It was covered by five thick V-shaped plates which almost enclosed the broad, cross-ridged areas where food collected by the arms was taken to the mouth. Small plates that covered those areas and the mouth (which was on top of the body) are almost always missing from fossils.

Most blastoids lived in colonies under shallow, quiet seas. Their jointed stalks broke to pieces soon after death, but their bodies frequently remained intact and collected in low spots. Great numbers are sometimes found in pockets of weathered Mississippian limestone.

If blastoid colonies suggest submarine flower beds, crinoids imply whole gardens. Although they began on a small scale in Ordovician seas, they prospered during the Silurian, Devonian, and Mississippian Periods, and again in the Permian. Mississippian crinoid banks must have covered acres of sea bottom. If living species are reliable guides, colours ranged from whitish to yellow, pink, red, lavender, and deep blue.

Eight hundred species of crinoids are living today, and many of them are abundant. Since they live in water 600 to 15,000 feet deep, however, they are among the least familiar of the ocean's inhabitants.

Crinoids may have dwelt in depths for ages, or they may have retreated to deep, dark, cold waters within the last 50 or 60 million years. The latter theory is suggested by the fact that many modern crinoids have become very different from any that lived in ancient seas which spread over continents. The group called feather stars even lose their stalks as they grow, swim at depths of 3500 to 4500 feet, and sometimes rise to the surface and rest among rocks near shore.

Feather stars are interesting, but they are not typical. As a typical crinoid we may choose *Megistocrinus evansi*, from Mississippian beds at Burlington. Its cup-shaped body was covered with thick plates; the arms branched several times; each branch once bore many delicate branchlets that are sometimes preserved in fossils. The jointed stalk divided into rootlike structures that grew over and even into the mud. They anchored *Megistocrinus* to the sea bottom but—unlike the roots of plants—they did not soak up water or mineral matter.

Megistocrinus was a typical crinoid, but there were many variations from its basic plan. Some crinoids developed deep, vase-shaped bodies; others became so small that we wonder how they managed to build stalks and arms. Some arms were reduced to mere stubs, a few expanded like sheets of chain mail, and others looked like jointed claws or spread into small, stony umbrellas. Stalks grew long or shortened into mere stubs; roots became plated bulbs or massive anchors; some disappeared from crinoids that clung to other things by means of branches from the stalks. One crinoid lost both

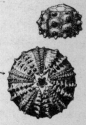

Keyhole urchin   (Arrows point to ambulacra)   Symmetrical urchin

Heart urchin

Three types of sea urchins

Clypeaster aegypticus, a very thick-shelled sea urchin. Its spines were short and thin.

roots and stalk, but was buoyed up by its long, feathery arms. Vast schools of these creatures drifted in Late Cretaceous seas that extended from Kansas to western Wyoming. Their fossils literally fill thin layers of limestone.

Starfish and Sea Urchins

Stalked echinoderms kept their mouths directed upward, even when they lost their stalks. Stalkless starfish and their kin reversed that position, and so did sea urchins.

Starfish apparently began when a Cambrian animal that was shaped like a flattened ball rolled over and began to eat things that lay or crept on the mud. In time the ball began to bulge in five places, along the grooves that gathered food. When the Ordovician Period began, descendants of these bulging balls had become animals shaped like plump versions of our conventional star. Since Middle Ordovician times, typical starfish have had five or more pointed rays, each containing a branch of the stomach and other internal organs. The mouth still opens at the centre of the undersurface, there is no front or rear to the body, and the animal crawls with fleshy tube "feet" that extend from the underside of the rays. Long tubes at the tip of each ray feel for food or taste it in the sea water.

Starfish feed in several ways, but only one is shown by fossils.

These particular animals crawled onto clams, took hold of the shells with their tube feet, and pulled. As they did so, the starfish secreted a liquid which made the clams relax. When their shells opened, starfish stomachs flowed over them and digested their flesh. Ordinarily, the meal was completed and the starfish crawled away. But when mud or sand settled quickly and deeply, the hungry animals were buried while they lay on the shells of their prey.

The starfish body is flexible, but the shell of plates that covers a typical sea urchin is not. It is a rigid and sometimes very thick structure that keeps its maker in one definite shape.

Some early sea urchins resembled cantaloupes in form; others had the proportions of doorknobs but were covered with tubercles. In fossils these seem ornamental; during life, they were bases for the attachment of spines that ranged from long, slender needles to thick clublike or even bottle-shaped structures. In some forms, the tips of the spines spread so broadly that they must have fitted together in a second coat around the shell.

All sea urchins show five double rows of plates containing holes through which tube feet now extend. These ambulacra correspond to the grooves on the underside of a starfish, though they show best on the urchin's upper surface and may not extend beyond it. The sea urchin's mouth, like that of the starfish, is on its underside.

Many sea urchins had—and still have—shells in which the ambulacra are alike in size and position, dividing the shell into equal parts. In other shells, one ambulacrum extends forward and the others are arranged in pairs on either side. The former group are the urchins that have long spines or thick ones; modern hatpin urchins use them to repel possible spines or thick ones; modern hatpin urchins use them to repel possible attackers. The animal's skin is sensitive to light and shade; when a shadow falls upon an urchin, it promptly turns its spines in that direction. We may assume that ancient long-spined urchins shared this habit and had spines that caused stinging pain.

Sea urchins with right and left sides have short spines that often look like hair. The shells, however, may be large and thick, with internal plates and bars that give extra strength. That is especially true of the cake urchins, which range from 3 to 7 inches in length, and whose ambulacra look like petals. These big urchins are common and very attractive fossils in Tertiary rocks of North America, though some of the finest specimens come from the vicinity of Cairo, Egypt.

Sand dollars are very thin sea urchins whose shells are almost flat on the underside. They, too, are strengthened by rods and plates, which leave very little space for the internal organs. Especially thin species are pierced by narrow holes. Sand dollars crawl on sand or in it. Most of the living species are found near the coasts of North America and Japan. Fossils are commonest in Cenozoic deposits near the Pacific coast, though they also are found in the South and East. One Ice-age, or Pleistocene, species is still the commonest living sand dollar from Mexico to Alaska.

8   FROM FINS TO LEGS
AND LAND

WHILE TRILOBITES crawled and horn-shells caught them, important events took place in fresh waters and on adjacent lands. Though these events brought death to uncounted creatures, they finally led to the evolution of four-legged animals that could live on land.

No one knows just where this change took place, but its site may have been a land that included northern Europe and apparently stretched westward to Greenland. Some books call it the Continent of the Old Red Sandstone after its most famous formation. The "Old Red" actually is a series of sandstones, conglomerates, marls, and lavas that accumulated throughout most of the Devonian Period. On the time scale we are using, its oldest beds settled some 400 million years ago, and its youngest no less than 350 million.

The Old Red Continent was a land of high, rugged mountain ranges separated by valleys or basins into which lavas sometimes poured from fissures as well as volcanoes. The climate was warm to tropical; dry seasons alternated with wet ones in which cloudbursts turned dried-up streams into torrents and filled valleys with shallow lakes. Water-dwellers prospered while the rains lasted but died by millions when drought reduced rivers and lakes to foul pools and expanses of sun-baked sand and mud.

In spite of these rigorous conditions, both fish and fishlike creatures were common. The latter belonged to the group called agnaths, whose name—it means "jawless ones"—describes their simple, slitlike mouths. *Cephalaspis*, one of the best-known agnaths of the Old Red times, had a solid, bony shield on the head and a flexible coat of plates and

Fossil and a restoration of a bone-covered ostracoderm. This primitive fishlike creature lived near the mouth of a Devonian river in what now is Wyoming. Princeton University.

scales that extended to the tip of the tail. The head-shield covered a bony skull which contained eyes, brain, nerves, and gills that breathed oxygen from water. The rest of the skeleton consisted of cartilage, or gristle, which vanished soon after the creature died. The tail bore a fin and so did the back, but two finlike structures behind the head seem to have been mere flaps of flesh covered by skin and scales. Paired fins and jaws apparently came into existence when agnaths evolved into fish.

That took place before Devonian times, for fish of several types were common in Old Red lakes and streams. Some were small, spiny creatures; others resembled armoured agnaths but had one pair of stiff, bone-covered fins. Still others were normally fish-shaped creatures with bones inside their bodies as well as protective plates and scales.

These ancient fish also had gills, as do their modern relatives. Those gills, however, were not too important, for many Old Red fish had lungs and used them to breathe oxygen from air, not from water. By this means, members of

Number 1, *Cephalaspis* and 2, *Pteraspis*, two armoured agnaths of the Old Red Sandstone. Number 3 is an armoured fish from the same formation.

two groups lived through dry seasons during which other fish and agnaths died.

One of these groups was made up of "true" lungfish, by which we mean creatures like those to which the name is given today. The nearest relatives of Old Red lungfish now live in parts of Australia where droughts still occur every year. Even when water is plentiful, however, Australian lungfish swim to the surface, stick out their snouts, and take in air. Lungfish of the Old Red probably shared this habit, and they surely inhaled air when ponds and streams became shallow and lost oxygen through the decay of dead fish and plants. Perhaps the creatures could even survive for a while in mud, as their living relatives do when water disappears.

Lungfish, however, were too highly specialized *as lungfish* to get away from water and mud, even briefly. Lungfish also were unable to produce descendants that would be creatures

Lungfish and fringe-fin. Number 1, *Dipterus*, a primitive lungfish rising to the surface to breathe air. Number 2, one tooth of *Dipterus*. Number 3, *Osteolepis*, an active predaceous fringe-fin of the Old Red Sandstone.

Number 1, bones in the long, flexible fin of a lungfish. Numbers 2–3, bones in the fin of a fringe-finned fish and an amphibian. Letters indicate identical bones in a forefin of the former and foreleg of the latter.

of any other sort. These changes could only be made by fish that breathed air and had three other qualifications which no true lungfish possessed.

First of these qualifications was a primitive set of bones in skull, jaw, and skeleton. Lungfish had developed too many skull bones and then had turned part of them into cartilage. Some bones in the jaw, as well as the skeleton, had also become cartilaginous.

Second among essential qualifications was a set of pointed teeth. Lungfish had lost the teeth from their jaws; those that remained on the roof of the mouth were broad plates fit only to crush hard-shelled food.

Third came fins with short, sturdy basal lobes containing muscles and bones that could—and would—become the framework of legs and feet. The rest of the fin was a fringe of small bones connected by skin. It could—and would—disappear. The lungfish fin was long, flexible, and leaflike, with soft "bones" that could not have turned into the skeleton of a leg.

Professor Alfred S. Romer of Harvard has outlined the steps by which fringe-finned fish and some of their

A Devonian fringe-finned fish begins to crawl overland to find
water. In the distance, a fish that cannot crawl struggles on mud
before dying.

descendants became four-legged animals. When drought
shrank streams and lakes into pools, both fringe-fins and
lungfish took refuge in them. For a while they got along
equally well, but when pools became mudholes only fringe-
fins could struggle out by means of their fin-lobes and creep
across low ground in a frantic effort to find other pools.
Those that did so plunged into water and lived; if they
possessed especially long, muscular fin-lobes, they also had a
chance to pass that character on to their offspring.

Here we pause to make a clear distinction between what
those fringe-finned fish were trying to do and the ultimate
result of their efforts. The fish *were not* trying to live on land,
nor were they making an effort to turn their fins into legs.
They *were* blindly leaving places where there was no water,
and were equally blindly going toward places where a little
water remained. Those that found such pools went no farther
unless the pool was already overcrowded, or unless it, too,
became dry. If it did, refugees repeated their struggle to find
more water in which they could and would remain fish.

We add those words "and would" for good reason, since no
fish big enough to make its way to water ever developed legs.

Ichthyostega, a primitive amphibian with legs and feet but a fishlike fin on its tail. This creature lived in Greenland about 345 million years ago.

But as millions of dry and then wet seasons passed, some fish whose fin-lobes had taken them to water produced offspring whose lobes were longer, with sturdier muscles and bones. When these offspring also lived through droughts, the process was repeated. In time it produced a new sort of creature that had lost its fin fringes, but whose lobes had grown into legs and feet with toes.

We have traced this one series of changes, but they did not take place alone. With them came modifications in size, skull, and skeleton—modifications which added up to a new class of animals, which we call amphibians. Their modern representatives include newts, salamanders, frogs, and toads.

Some theorists have pictured early amphibians as creatures that strove to spend their whole lives on land. For 40 million years, however, they were defeated by soft eggs that had to develop in water, and by young that could breathe only with plume-shaped gills like those of a newly hatched fringe-fin. But at last some unwittingly creative female did away with these obstacles. She laid eggs that would hatch into young whose lungs could be used at once. She also wrapped those eggs in membranes filled with liquid that took the place of

Seymouria, a link between amphibians and reptiles that lived in Texas during Early Permian times. At the right is a petrified reptilian egg, also of Permian age.

water and covered them with tough shells. Thus equipped, her progeny became reptiles and truly terrestrial quadrupeds.

This story is direct and dramatic; it also seems to be untrue. The oldest known amphibian gives no hint of being a thwarted land-dweller; it is a fish-shaped creature about 4 feet long that had awkward, sprawling legs and a tail with fins. If these structures mean anything, they tell us that the animal swam happily through lakes and rivers in what is now Greenland and went ashore only when he had to do so. Perhaps, he, too, was beset by dry seasons that turned his home waters into mud.

That, however, is supposition; we know little about the climate of Greenland in Late Devonian and Early Mississippian times. But we do know that while amphibians supposedly strove to become land-dwellers, most of those that are known actually evolved into aquatic swimmers. We know, too, that most reptiles, when they appeared, also spent their adult lives in streams, lakes, and swamps.

Does that seem strange? Not when we consider the evidence furnished by fossils. Fringe-finned fish were aquatic carnivores that fed on other fish. Early amphibians were carnivorous too; besides fish, their diet soon included other amphibians. The first reptiles also seem to have been meateaters, yet Early Pennsylvanian forests were inhabited only by millipedes, spiders, insects, and a few small amphibians. What could reptiles do except live in the water and feed on fish, amphibians, and smaller or more sluggish reptiles?

But why should any water-dweller lay eggs that could develop on land and hatch into lung-breathing young ones?

Again Professor Romer offers a plausible theory. As soon as amphibians began they prospered; in 30 million years or so, they and fish must have made great demands on available supplies of food. Moreover, eggs laid in water were likely to be eaten, and so were tadpoles that might hatch from them. There also remained the threat of dry seasons, even though they were not as severe as they had been during Old Red times. Any vertebrate which laid eggs that could develop on land freed both eggs and newly hatched young from these dangers.

If Romer is right, egg-laying on land became established because it gave this selective advantage over egg-laying in water. When a few young ones began to stay on land, they too profited by freedom from hungry neighbours. Once some reptiles established themselves on land, others were able to prey on them, and so the cycle progressed. Long before the Pennsylvanian Period, or Coal Age, ended there were reptiles 5 to 8 feet long that could not have lived in water if they had wanted to do so.

These creatures were highly specialized, but one "missing link" between amphibians and reptiles lived on through millions of years into the Permian Period. Its remains were buried in red shaly deposits of north-central Texas, and have been named *Seymouria* for the county seat near which they were found.

Some experts call *Seymouria* a very primitive reptile; others say he remained an amphibian. In either case, he was a short-legged, stocky, ugly quadruped about 20 inches in length. His skull was broad and flat on top, with bones essentially like those of more ancient aquatic amphibians. The short, thick legs sprawled sideways; the backbone was heavy and stiff; the tail, which was thick near its base, tapered abruptly to a point. The whole body was hardly built for swimming, but if *Seymouria* lived on land he crawled with his belly flat on the ground. Restorations usually show the male among simple ferns, while his mate rests sleepily near some tough-shelled, elongate eggs that are partly covered with sand. They imply that the creatures were reptiles. If *Seymouria* still belonged among amphibians, the eggs should be soft and covered with water.

9 LIFE AND DEATH ON DELTAS

WHILE FRINGED fins evolved into legs and amphibians produced reptiles, great changes took place on the earth. Shallow seas spread widely and then turned into land; land crumpled into mountains, and newly filled basins became swamps in which coal accumulated.

We should say that the *materials* of coal accumulated, for the stuff that settled in those swamps was dead trunks, stems, and leaves, mixed with fine mud and other sediment. As the dead plants settled, they slowly decayed into mucky peat and then into lignite, which was compressed into coal under the weight of rocks that settled on top of it. This part of the process usually took millions of years.

Coal swamps once were pictured as hot, steamy morasses where any animal that did not swim slithered over bottomless mud. This picture does not exaggerate the humidity, but the climate apparently was warm rather than intensely hot. It also was uniform, with little change from season to season or from one part of the world to another. This, in turn, allowed the same or very similar plants to grow from subpolar to equatorial regions and on every continent.

The largest of those plants were scale trees, which reached diameters of 4 to 6 feet and were 60 to 100 feet high. Leaves like broad, oversized pine needles grew directly from their trunks and branches. When the leaves fell off they left scars that still look like scales, thus giving the trees their everyday name. The only living relatives of scale trees are so-called ground pines and ground cedars, which creep under forests.

Vines clung to the trunks of scale trees, and ferns grew in their shade. Some kinds had leaves 6 feet long; others developed thick, woody stems 30 to 50 feet high. True ferns,

Some typical plants of a coal swamp. Number 1, several species of *Lepidodendron*, and 2, *Sigillaria*, both scale trees related to modern club mosses. Number 3, tree fern. Number 4, *Cordaites*, related to conifers. Number 5, several species of *Calamites*, which were ancient scouring rushes.

however, were out-numbered by seed ferns, which had
nutlike seeds at the tips of their leaves.

Horsetails, or scouring rushes, are now small plants that
live on either moist or dry, sunny ground. Horsetails of the
coal swamps grew in wet places or even in very shallow
water, reached heights of 30 feet and diameters of 12 to 14
inches. In many places they formed canebrakes much more
dense than the canebrakes of today.

Both amphibians and reptiles swam in coal swamps, and
the reptiles crept into forests when the time came to lay eggs.
As we have seen, this led to life on land and to the
development of purely terrestrial creatures 4 to 8 feet in
length that weighed 50 to 150 pounds.

In Europe, the time of great coal swamps is called the Late
Carboniferous or Coal Age and ranks as an epoch, not as a
period. In America, the Coal Age is usually called the
Pennsylvanian Period, though it may be bracketed with the
Mississippian as the Carboniferous Periods. We have done
this in Chapter 3.

Red Beds and Amphibians

It is often supposed that geologic periods end in upheavals,
eruptions, and other catastrophes. Such events did close the
Pennsylvanian, or Late Carboniferous, in Europe and Asia.
In much of North America, however, seas merely grew
shallow and disappeared. In the West, this was followed by
sinking that let a new sea spread from central Texas to
Nebraska and eastward to Ohio. In Kansas it became so salty
that little or nothing could live in it and rock salt settled on its
bottom. In northern Texas, however, sea water was replaced
by new Permian land.

That word "new" is appropriate, for this land was a
complex series of deltas built by rivers that brought mud
from mountains to the east and south, and deposited it in dark
red beds. Though some nearby regions had long dry seasons,
deltas on which the Red Beds settled were crisscrossed by

Eryops (above) was a Permian amphibian 5 to 7 feet long. On the bottom are three individuals of bony-headed *Diplocaulus.*

rivers that kept lowland forests moist and often spread into swamps. They allowed both amphibians and reptiles to live in water, on land, or in the damp zone between them.

Permian amphibians ranged from small mud-grubbers to big, predatory carnivores. Chief among the latter was *Eryops*, a plump, broad-bodied creature with short, massive legs, a strong swimming tail, and an over-all length of 5 to 7 feet. His skull was bony, rough, and massive; his jaws were set with sharp, conical teeth, and others grew from the roof of the mouth. *Eryops* probably fed largely on fish, which were common in swamps and streams of the deltas. His shape suggests that he also sunned himself on mudbanks, as alligators do today. *Eryops* must have stayed very close to the water, however, for he could not raise his body off the ground and run, as alligators and crocodiles do.

Small amphibians were more active but less dangerous. Sixteen-inch *Cacops* apparently crawled on land, though the ridge of bone along his back must have made him stiff and

Varanosaurus (1) and *Diadectes* (2), two reptiles of the Permian deltas. Number 3 is the stiff-backed amphibian *Cacops*.

awkward. Other amphibians were common in the region that is now northeastern Arizona. There beds of buff sandstone contain great numbers of footprints, many of which were made by creatures not much larger than *Cacops*.

Diplocaulus, of the Texas deltas, probably never went on land. This bizarre amphibian possessed a narrow, flattened body, a long swimming tail, and short, weak legs that must have been useless. The head, however, was a wide triangle of massive bone, with the mouth on the underside. *Diplocaulus* apparently grubbed for wormlike creatures that crawled on the bottoms of streams and swamps. Between meals the amphibian lay on mud in a state of near-unconsciousness that was deeper and lasted longer than sleep. The giant salamander of modern Japan spends most of its life in a similar state.

Reptiles of the Deltas

Land-dwelling reptiles seem to have begun with creatures much like *Seymouria* that lived in Middle Pennsylvanian forests. *Seymouria* itself was an inhabitant of the Red Bed deltas, as were many reptiles that neither looked nor acted like amphibians. One reptile that has been found in Oklahoma was 12 feet long and weighed about 730 pounds.

Meat-eaters of the deltas were more varied than herbivorous reptiles. One of the former was named *Varanosaurus* because it resembled modern monitor lizards, whose technical name is *Varanus*. Although *Varanosaurus* undoubtedly was a hunter, his hind legs could hardly lift his body from the ground. He must have lain in wait for prey, which he captured in short, scrambling attacks.

The largest meat-eaters of the deltas are called *Dimetrodon*. There were several species of these reptiles, and some of them lived in Texas before the Pennsylvanian Period closed. They departed as the Early Permian sea spread eastward; when it gave way to swamps their descendants returned in the form of new species 9 to 11 feet long that weighed as much as 670 pounds. Their name refers to teeth of two lengths; daggerlike stabbers at the front of the mouth and shorter cutting teeth along the sides.

Dimetrodon has been nicknamed the "tiger of the deltas." Like the tiger, he hid until his prey came near, but the jungles in which *Dimetrodon* waited consisted of horsetails, not grasses, and he rushed to the attack on the ground, not by leaping upon his victim. The ancient reptile also killed with his stabbing teeth, for he could not strike with his forelegs and feet.

Two kinds of teeth were *Dimetrodon*'s most significant possession, but his "fin" was the most puzzling. We are careful to put the word "fin" in quotes, for the structure actually was a web of skin stretched over tall, slender spines that grew upward from the back. On a reptile 11 feet long, the spines were as much as 4 feet high. Fossils show that many spines were broken. Some seem to have healed promptly, but others became diseased.

Number 1, the carnivorous finbacked reptile *Dimetrodon*, 9 to 11 feet long. Number 2, in the distance, is the plant-eater *Edaphosaurus*.

We can only guess how this dry-land, immovable fin was used. Some old books show *Dimetrodon* upside-down with the fin in water, where it served as a keel. Other books show only the spines, which supposedly looked like horsetail stems and so helped the big reptile hide in thickets. Another theory suggests that *Dimetrodon* used the fin to warm himself by sitting broadside to the sun on cool mornings. During hot afternoons, he could rest in the shade and use the fin as a radiator to get rid of heat if he had become too warm. Overheating is dangerous to reptiles, and *Dimetrodon* was too big to snuggle down among cool, dead leaves on the floor of the forest, as some tropical snakes do today.

The so-called fin was not found in *Dimetrodon* alone; it was developed and elaborated by a neighbour, *Edaphosaurus*. His spines, which were shorter and thicker than those of *Dimetrodon*, bore side branches that grew in pairs. A German paleontologist once suggested that these branches increased the resemblance to horsetails, but another German thought the spines made *Edaphosaurus* too prickly to be attacked. The latter theory overlooks the big teeth and strong jaws of *Dimetrodon*, as well as injuries to spines and other bones of *Edaphosaurus*. To *Dimetrodon*, the other reptile must have been little more than 350 to 600 pounds of unprotected meat.

Unprotected? Yes, for *Edaphosaurus* was a peaceful eater of clams, snails, and plants. This diet is indicated by the blunt teeth in his jaws and by broad plates on the floor and roof of his mouth. These plates, which were studded with buttonlike teeth, crushed shells readily but could not have been used in a fight.

Some reptiles always look sullen or even malignant; *Dimetrodon* probably did so. Though not a reptile, *Eryops* was almost as forbidding. Varanosaurs combined the alertness of relatively small hunters with apparent eagerness to kill.

Still, life on the Permian deltas probably was no more savage than life in almost any other region at almost any other time. There were plant-eaters, fish-eaters, mud-grubbers, and clam-eaters; there were creatures that hunted for food and others that let it come within reach of their jaws. Few meals were more bloody than a modern tiger's or leopard's, and no Permian reptile was as savage-looking as a Gaboon viper or as deadly as a large rattlesnake.

In short, both life and death on the Permian deltas were normal or even sluggish. They remained so until climatic changes turned the Southwest into deserts of wind-blown sand.

10 MUSEUMS AND BOOKS

FOSSILS CAN BE read about and studied in pictures, but they should also be seen. A great number of museums in the British Isles display collections of fossils.

In London there is the *British Museum (Natural History)*, South Kensington, with many galleries devoted to fossil vertebrates and explanatory exhibits of invertebrates and plants. The fossil mammal gallery and the pleiosaurs and ichthyosaurs are particularly worth seeing, and there is an educational section which exists to help young paleontologists. The *Institute of Geological Sciences* (formerly *Geological Survey and Museum*), also in South Kensington, has exhibits explaining the local geology and fossils of the different parts of Great Britain.

The *Sedgwick Museum*, Cambridge, has extensive displays, mainly, but not entirely, of invertebrate fossils.

The *Royal Scottish Museum*, Edinburgh, is noteworthy for exhibits illustrating Scottish rocks and fossils; Devonian fish are especially well represented. The *Hunterian Museum*, Glasgow, also has an excellent collection of Scottish rocks and fossils. Many Jurassic marine reptiles are also preserved here.

The *National Museum of Wales*, Cardiff, has a large display of Welsh geology and fossils.

In Ireland the two most important museums are the *Ulster Museum*, Belfast, which concentrates on material from Northern Ireland and the *National Museum of Ireland*, Dublin, with collections from the whole of Ireland.

Among the larger cities of England several have excellent displays of local geology including: *Bristol City Museum, City of Birmingham Museum, City of Liverpool Museum, City of Leeds Museum*, the *Manchester Museum*, (which is particularly noteworthy,) the *Hancock Museum*, Newcastle-on-Tyne, the *Nottingham Natural History Museum*, the *University Museum*, Oxford, *Norwich Castle Museum*, and the *Yorkshire Museum*, York.

Outside the major cities some smaller museums have displays which are well worth seeing, of which the following are outstanding: The *Dartford Borough Museum*, Dartford, Kent (mainly for Pleistocene mammalia and implements); the *Dorest County Museum*, Dorchester (Jurassic and Cretaceous invertebrates and reptiles); the *Dudley Museum*, Dudley, Worcs. (excellent Silurian fossils from the local outcrops); *Elgin Museum*, Morayshire (Triassic reptiles); *Ipswich Museum*, Suffolk (Pleistocene mammals and invertebrates); *Ludlow Museum*, Shropshire (fossils from Shropshire); *Lyme Regis Museum*, Dorset (for local, and very important, Jurassic and Cretaceous fossils); *Sandown Museum*, Isle of Wight, with important collections of Mesozoic and Tertiary fossils from the classic geological area of the Isle of Wight; *Scunthorpe Borough Museum*, Lincs., with important local collections; *Torquay Natural History Society Museum*, Devon, with Devonian fossils and Pleistocene mammals from the local cave deposits. The *Whitby Museum*, Yorkshire, has very important collections of local Jurassic fossils, including marine reptiles.

In southern and eastern Africa there are important collections of fossils at the *South African Museum (Natural History)*, Capetown (particularly Triassic and Pleistocene vertebrates); the *Transvaal Museum*, Pretoria (important collections of *Australopithecus*); the *Orange Free State National Museum*, Bloemfontein (Pleistocene mammals); the *Uganda Museum*, Kampala (Tertiary vertebrates); and the *National Museum*, Nairobi (Tertiary and Pleistocene mammals and australopithecines from Olduvai Gorge).

In Australia there are important collections of fossils on display at the *Australia Museum*, Sydney (vertebrate fossils), the *Australian National Museum*, Melbourne, the *Western Australia Museum*, Perth, and the *Queensland Museum*, Brisbane.

In New Zealand the most important displays of fossils are at the *Auckland Institute Museum*, Auckland, the *Dominion Museum*, Wellington, the *Canterbury Museum*, Christchurch, the *Otago Museum*, Otago, the *Dunedin Museum*, Dunedin, the *Napier Museum*, Napier, and the *Invercargill Museum*, Invercargill.

BOOKS

Books about fossils range from very simple volumes for children to technical treatises. A good textbook of earth history, with much about fossils, is *Historical Geology*, second edition, by Carl O. Dunbar (London: John Wiley, 1960). *The Vertebrate Story*, by Alfred S. Romer (London: University of Chicago Press, 1959) is a popular account of the evolution of the vertebrates by the most eminent living American authority. *Introducing Geology. The Earth's Crust Considered as History* by D. V. Ager (London: Faber & Faber, 1961) is a readable account of geological history, centered on the geology of the British Isles. *The Evolution of Life* by F. H. T. Rhodes (Penguin Books, Harmondsworth, 1962) is an accurate and well illustrated introduction to paleontology. *Fossils* by H. H. Swinnerton (Collins, 1960) (New Naturalist series) is readable, and devoted mainly to British forms.

Readers who want to identify British fossils will find most of the more common forms very well illustrated in *British Palaeozoic Fossils* (second edition, 1966), *British Mesozoic Fossils* (second edition, 1964), and *British Caenozoic Fossils* (second edition, 1963) (published by the Trustees of the *British Museum* (Natural History)).

The geology of England, Scotland, and Wales is well covered in an introductory way by the series *British Regional Geology*, issued by the Institute of Geological Sciences.

History of Paleontology.

Human beings took a long time to admit that fossils once were alive, and still longer to realize their meaning. Several books tell portions of this story:

Fenton, C. L. and M. A. Fenton. *Giants of Geology* (London: W. H. Allen, 1952). Chapters 2, 7, 10, 13, 16, 17 deal with fossils and men who discovered them.

Miller, Hugh. *The Old Red Sandstone* (various editions and dates). Miller was a great collector and a fine writer; this, his most famous book, was a scientific best seller for many years, and its influence extended into the 1900s.

Moore, R. E. *Man, Time and Fossils* (London: Jonathan Cape, 1953). The evolutionary story told by fossils, traced in the work of outstanding paleontologists.

Books Describing Fossils

Augusta, J. *A Book of Mammoths* (London: Paul Hamlyn, 1962); *Prehistoric Animals* (same 1960); *Prehistoric Reptiles and Birds* (same 1961); *Prehistoric Sea Monsters* (same 1964). Handsome volumes illustrated, partly in colour, by Z. Burian. They contain many restorations not found elsewhere, and their short texts provide a surprising amount of information.

Colbert, E. H. *Dinosaurs* (London: Hutchinson, 1961). This is the most up-to-date and comprehensive book about dinosaurs now available in English. *The Age of Reptiles*, by the same author (London: Weidenfeld & Nicolson, 1965) deals with the dinosaurs and also with all the other contemporary reptile groups.

Fenton, C. L. and M. A. Fenton. *The Fossil Book* (London: W. H. Allen). A large but non-technical book for adults, abundantly illustrated. It traces the history of life, at the same time describing the principal groups of plants and animals. Many important species are illustrated and named.

Glaessner, M. F. *"Pre-Cambrian Animals,"* *Scientific American*, Vol. 204 (March 1961), pp. 72—78. Not a book, but an article that describes and illustrates Late Precambian animals of Australia.

Simpson, G. G. *Horses* (London: Oxford University Press, 1951). A general and authoritative semi-technical book on horses and their relatives.

Ancient Man

Augusta, J. *Prehistoric Man* (London: Paul Hamlyn, 1960). Like other books written by Professor Augusta and illustrated by Z. Burian, this handsome volume contains many unusual restorations. Its account of Czech mammoth hunters is especially useful.

Cornwall, I. W. *The Making of Man* (London: Phoenix House, 1960). This children's book offers a compact survey of ancient man and his predecessors which may be used by anyone. The author is an eminent British prehistorian.

Dart, R. A. and D. Craig. *Adventures with the Missing Link* (London: Hamish Hamilton, 1959). Professor Dart's own account of his work with man-apes and his ideas about them.

Howells, W. *Mankind in the Making* (London: Secker & Warburg, 1960). A non-technical survey emphasizing skeletal remains, not tools.

Leaky, L. S. B. *"Finding the World's Earliest Man."* *National Geographic*, Vol. 118 (September 1960), pp. 420-35. *"Exploring 1,750,000 Years into Man's Past."* Same, Vol. 120 (October 1961), pp. 564-89. *"Adventures in the Search for Man."* Same, Vol. 123 (January 1963), pp. 132-52. Superbly illustrated accounts of the Leakeys' discoveries. The second article deals with apes and ape-men.

Books for Boys and Girls

Rhodes, F. T. H., Zim, H. S. and Shaffer, P. R. *Fossils, a Guide to Prehistoric Life* (London: Paul Hamlyn, 1965). This is an excellent, readable and surprisingly detailed introduction to fossils, with many coloured illustrations.

Swinton W. E. *The Story of Prehistoric Animals* (London: Rathbone Books, 1961). A very attractive book, with the main emphasis on vertebrates.

Casanova, R. *Fossil Collecting: An Illustrated Guide* (London: Faber & Faber, 1960). Describes how fossils are classified, the geological time scale, and where they can be found, with localities.

Oakley, K. P. and Muir-Wood, H. M. *The Succession of Life through Geological Time (British Museum (Natural History)* sixth edition, 1964). A good guide to the history of life.

Zim, H. S. *Dinosaurs* (London: World's Work, 1963). Gives reconstructions of most of the known types of dinosaurs and also discusses their probable habits.

Fenton, C. L. *Tales Told By Fossils: From Dinosaurs to Man* (London: Carousel Books 1974). This 2nd volume carries on the story of fossils from lizard-hipped dinosaurs to Neanderthal man.

GLOSSARY

Abbevillian. A name which, in Europe, has replaced *Chellean.* The latter is still used in Africa.

Adaptation. Any structure or function that fits a living thing to its surroundings or way of life.

Agnaths. Primitive fishlike creatures that had no jaws and apparently no paired fins.

Algae. A great variety of simple plants and plantlike things such as seaweeds.

Amber. Fossil resin from ancient trees; it often contains insects.

Ammonoids. Extinct cephalopods whose shells contain bent or crumpled septa. Ammonoids were commonest in the Mesozoic Era.

Amphibians. Vertebrates that usually have four legs, lay soft eggs that develop in water, and breathe with gills while they are young. Some highly specialized forms have lost one or more of these characteristics. Frogs and salamanders are typical amphibians.

Ape-man. Same as *Pithecanthropus.*

Apes. This term usually means anthropoid apes, which are manlike mammals that still do not walk erect, talk, or possess brains as large as those of human beings. Teeth, skull, jaws, and bones of the hips and limbs also differ from those of man.

Australopithecus. Small man-apes of Early Ice-age Africa.

Barrier. Any natural feature that keeps living things from spreading to other parts of the earth. The sea is a barrier to land animals; mountains are barriers to lowland creatures.

Belemnoids. Extinct torpedo-or dart-shaped cephalopods with ten arms and small shells and other hard parts that were covered by skin.

Bird-hips. Ornithischian dinosaurs.

Birds. Feathered vertebrates whose forelegs have become wings.

Blastoids. Echinoderms with stalks and nutlike or bud-shaped bodies covered by a few thick plates.

Bone. One of the parts of a vertebrate skeleton, even if it consists of cartilage. Also the hard material of bones.

Brachiopods. Marine animals whose shells have two parts, or valves, which never are similar. Bodies differ greatly from those of clams.

Calcite. Limy material found in corals, shells, crinoids, and so on. It is identical with the principal material in limestone.

Carbonization. Incomplete decay that leaves the carbon that was once in leaves, flesh, skin, and so on. Many fossil plants have been carbonized; so have some fish and reptiles.

Carnivores. In general, animals that eat meat or other animals. The carnivores (or Carnivora), however, are a group of meat-eating mammals that have four or five toes on each foot and sharp teeth, and usually—but not always—possess claws.

Cartilage. Soft, translucent material found in many vertebrate skeletons. As animals grow old, cartilage may be replaced by bone.

Cell. A small structure made up of living material; also the wall of hard, often woody material that may cover it.

Cephalopods. Highly developed molluscs with large eyes and horny beaks surrounded by fleshy arms that catch food.

Chellean. An ancient stage or type of tool-making, characterized by crudely chipped knives, scrapers, and blunt "hand axes," which probably were used to dig roots, skin large animals, ànd chop meat. Later hand axes were more carefully chipped and were pointed at one end.

Chromosomes. Structures which contain the genes, or tiny particles, that control heredity. Fossil chromosomes are very rare.

Corals. Soft-bodied marine animals that often build stony supports. Corals are often, but wrongly, called insects.

Crinoids. Echinoderms with many plates on the body and prominent arms that usually branch. Most crinoid bodies are attached to the top of jointed stalks.

Cystoids. Primitive echinoderms whose bodies usually are covered with many small plates. Most cystoids possess stalks.

Dinosaurs. Two groups (orders) of Mesozoic reptiles, many of which became very large. See *Saurischians* and *Ornithischians.*

Echinoderms. Marine animals whose skins contain plates or spines of calcite. Crinoids, starfish, and sea urchins are echinoderms.

Environment. The surroundings of living things, including other animals and plants.

Evolution. The process by which living things change their hereditary appearance, structure, or functions. In time these changes produce new varieties, species, and larger groups.

Extinction. Any process that causes a species or some other group of living things to die out.

Fish. Three large groups, or classes, of water-dwelling vertebrates. Fish have jaws and fins that are arranged in pairs, as well as others on the back, underside, and tail.

"Forams" (actually foraminifers). One-celled protozoans whose soft bodies are protected by hard cases or shells.

Formation. A series of beds or strata that are essentially similar and settled during a limited part of geologic time. Beds in one formation usually contain many identical fossils.

Fossils. Remains or traces of things that lived during ancient geologic times and were buried in rocks that accumulated on the earth's outer portion, or crust.

Ganglion. A cluster or mass of nerve cells that both receives and sends out messages without passing them on to the brain.

Genus. A group of related and generally similar species. To avoid repetition, genera are sometimes referred to as "types."

Gills. Fringed, feathery, or layered organs used to breathe in water. Gills developed at various times and in several ways in different groups of animals.

Herbivores. Plant-eating animals, chiefly vertebrates.

Horn-shells. A non-technical name for cephalopods that build shells around their bodies; the nautiloids and ammonoids.

Ice Age. When capitalized, this term means the Pleistocene Epoch. There were, however, other epochs of cold and glaciation.

Index fossil. A fossil found in the rocks of one epoch or smaller division of time. Once the sequence of rocks and their time-divisions is known, such fossils indicate the geologic age of the beds or formations in which they occur.

Isolation. Anything that separates living things from their relatives or from immigrants. Creatures that are isolated for a long time usually evolve into unusual species and larger groups.

Land bridges. Strips of land that extend between continents or large islands. These strips usually rise at some times and sink at others, thus changing from bridges to barriers.

Larva. An early stage of an animal; it can move about, feed, and do other things, but it is different from adults. A caterpillar is the larva of a butterfly or moth; a tadpole is a larval or toad.

Ligament. A band or sheet of tough material that fastens one vertebrate structure to another. Ligaments that connected vertebrae of bird-hipped dinosaurs were stiffened by limy material and therefore are found in fossils.

Lizard-hips. Saurischian dinosaurs.

Living fossils. Living things that have not changed much during periods or even eras and usually are plentiful today.

Lungfish. Fish with lungs and narrow, very flexible paired fins. Many bones in the skeleton have become cartilage; others in the jaws and skull have been lost, and so have ordinary teeth. Lungfish are highly specialized and are not the ancestors of amphibians.

Mammals. Four-limbed vertebrates with warm blood and hair; the females produce milk from glands in the skin. Fossil mammals are recognized by features of their skulls, skeletons, and teeth. Each half of the lower jaw, for example, contains only one bone, though reptilian jaws have several bones.

Mammoths. Extinct elephants of the Pleistocene, or Ice Age. They had high skulls and very long tusks; at least one species was covered with coarse hair and fine wool.

Man. A human being. Some scientists define man as the only tool-making animal. Others list characters that include a large brain, a short face without a projecting muzzle, teeth that are small for the size of the skull, and hip and limb bones adapted to upright life on the ground.

Man-apes. Early Pleistocene creatures that combined the upright position of man with apelike skulls and small brains. Habits probably were manlike.

Mastodons. Mammals closely related to elephants, but with less specialized teeth. One species, the American mastodon, died out only a few thousand years ago.

Molluscs. Clams, oysters, snails, and their relatives. Most of them have shells, but the octopus and some snails do not.

Muscles. Organs that produce movement by shortening the fibres of which they are composed. Most ancient muscles are traced by marks which they left on shells or bones.

Nautiloids. Molluscs whose shells are built on the plan seen in shells of *Nautilus*. Nautiloids were most abundant during the Paleozoic Era.

Neanderthal man. An ancient human species characterized by a long, low skull, chinless face, and heavy bones in arms and legs. These people lived in many regions during the Pleistocene Epoch.

Organism. A plant, animal, or any other living thing.

Ornithischians. Dinosaurs whose hipbones resemble those of birds.

Paleontology. The science that deals with fossils.

Paranthropus. A group, or genus, of large man-apes that liked lake shores and moist plains. *Paranthropus* lived in Africa during Early Pleistocene times.

Pithecanthropus. A genus of erect but rather small-brained men of apelike appearance that ranged from Africa to Europe, China, and Java during the Middle Pleistocene. They made stone tools, including those of Chellean, or Abbevillian, type. Often called *Homo erectus*.

Proconsul. A genus of Early Miocene apes of Africa; they seem to have been the ancestors of chimpanzees and gorillas as well as man-apes.

Protozoans. One-celled creatures often called "first animals," though they seem to belong to other kingdoms. Most fossil protozoans are "forams."

Red Beds. When capitalized, this term means delta deposits of Late Pennsylvanian and Early Permian age in Texas and Oklahoma. However, dark-red sands and muds were deposited at other times and in other regions. Thus there are Devonian red beds (usually not capitalized) in Pennsylvania, Triassic red beds in New England, and so on.

Reptiles. Vertebrates with bony skeletons and dry, usually scaly skins. Eggs develop on land or in mother's body; the young breathe with lungs, not gills. Teeth usually have only one point; each half of the lower jaw contains more than one bone, in contrast to the jaw of mammals.

Saurischians. Dinosaurs whose hipbones resemble those of lizards and crocodiles. Saurischians include the largest dinosaurs.

Segment. Part of a body that is marked off or separated from parts before and behind. An earthworm has many similar segments; those of trilobites may be similar or may differ in size or shape.

Septum. A dividing wall or partition. In this book the term refers to partitions built behind the bodies of horn-shelled cephalopods.

Shell. The hard covering of a body or structure. In this book the word is used for hard coverings that cannot be shed and replaced by a new one. A horn-shell is a good example.

Skin-crust. A covering formed upon the skin of an animal. It can be shed and replaced by a new one; a crab's "shell" is an example. Many skin-crusts never become hard.

Species. One kind of living thing. A group of similar species that are related makes up a genus.

Spore. A cell that can develop into a new living thing without being fertilized or combining with a different cell. Spores are especially important among plants such as ferns.

Suture. The line along which two hard parts join. The sutures of horn-shells show where septa join the shells.

Thecodonts. Extinct reptiles that were the ancestors of lizard-hipped and bird-hipped dinosaurs, as well as phytosaurs. Thecodonts or closely related reptiles also were the ancestors of crocodiles, pterosaurs, and birds.

Thorax. The part of an animal behind its head or a headlike section such as the cephalon of a trilobite.

Trilobites. Extinct animals whose bodies were made up of jointed sections and were divided into *lobes* by grooves that ran lengthwise across the segments. The name means "three-lobed ones."

Vertebrates. In everyday language, vertebrates are animals with backbones or series of vertebrae. Actually, some vertebrae are only partly formed; many consist of cartilage, not bone; others are not preserved in fossils. Some scientists call an animal a vertebrate if it has a skull or a case of bone or cartilage around the brain. Another name for such animals is *craniates*.

Zinjanthropus. A large African man-ape with powerful jaw muscles, indicated by a crest on top of the skull. The creature may belong to the genus *Paranthropus*.

INDEX

with pronunciations

Pronunciations of most names are given in the singular, even though the names themselves may be plural: Titanotheres (TY´ tan o THEER) for example. Exceptions are terms whose singular form differs considerably from the plural; for these the plural pronunciation is followed by the singular, as in Ganglia (GANG gli a; GANG gli on).

Some words have one pronunciation as formal names but another when they are turned into English. Formal names usually are italicized in text and are pronounced in "English" Latin: *Ammonites* (AM´ mo NY teez) for example. But the same name becomes ammonites (AM mon ites) in English.

Accidents 20
Adaption 35
Ages, Geologic, 27, 28, 29
    in years 28 — 30
Agnaths (AG nath) 19, 73, 74, 75, 76
Algae (AL jee; AL ga) 31, 33, 34, 41
Amber, fossils in 18, 24
Ambulacra (AM)
byu LA cra;
    AM´ byu LA crum) 69, 70, 71, 72
Ameura (a MYU ra) 46, 48
Ammonites (AM´ mo NY teez when
    italicized; otherwise AM mon ites)
    57
Ammonoids (AM mon oid) 53, 57 — 61
    "abberrant" 59, 60
    evolution 57, 58
    uncoiled 57, 59, 60
Amphibians, origin of 77, 85 —87
    primitive 77 — 82, 85 — 87

Bacteria
Baculites (BAK´ yu LY teez when
    italicized; otherwise BAK yu
    LITES) 58, 59, 60, 61
Behaviour 21
Belemnoids (BEL em noid) 21, 61, 62
Blastoids (Blass toid) 66, 68
Bone Cabin, Wyoming 9, 12, 31, 63
Borings, snail 22, 23
Brachiopods (BRAK´ i o pód) 20, 23,
    33, 36, 37
Brains 19, 20
Bryosoans 36
Bumastus (byu MASS tus) 46, 49, 52
Burlington, Iowa 63, 64, 69

Cacops (KAY kops) 86, 87
Calamites (KAL´ a MY teez) 84
Calymene (ka LIM´ e NEE) 50

Cambrian (KAM bri un) Period, 17, 29, 33, 35
    fossils 17, 27, 33, 36, 42, 45, 63
Carboniferous (KAR´ bon IF er us) Periods 29, 85
Cenozoic (SEE´ no ZOE ik) Era 28, 39, 72
Cephalaspis (SEF´ a LAS pis) 73, 75
Cephalon (SEF a lon) 44, 45, 50
Cephalopods (SEF a lo pod) 52 — 62
Chromosome (KRO mo soam) 18
Climates, ancient 10, 21, 73
Coal, origin 83, 84, 85
    swamps 83, 84, 85
Coal Age 21, 81, 85
Collecting 9, 11, 12, 13, 14, 63 — 65
    localities 9, 12, 63 — 65
Connecticut Valley Corals, colonial honeycomb 22
    horn 36, 37
    rugose 37
    structures 22, 23, 26, 36
Cordaites (KOR´ duh Y teez) 84
Cretaceous (kree TAY shus) Period 28, 53, 59, 62
Crinoidal (kry NOID al) limestone 64
Crinoids (KRY noid) 22, 63 — 67
    rootless 66
Cryptolithus (KRIP´ toe LITH us) 49
Cystoid (SIS toid) 64, 67

Dawn crinoid 67
"Devil's Corkscrew" 24
Devonaster 67
Devonian (de VOE ni un) Period 29, 51, 58, 68, 73
Diadectes (DY a DEK´ teez) 87
Dimetrodon (dy MET ro don) 88, 89, 90
Dipleura (dy PLOO rah) 50
Diplocaulus (DIP´ lo CAW lus) 86, 87
Dipterus 76
Disease 20, 23, 88

Echinoderms (e KY no derm) 65 — 72
Edaphosaurus (e DAF´ o SAW rus) 87, 90
Edrioaster (ED´ ri o AS ter) 67

Eggs, amphibian 79, 81, 82
    reptile 80, 81
Environments, ancient 20, 21
Eocene (EE o seen) Epoch 27, 28, 32, 62
Eryops (AIR i ops) 86, 90
Exogyra (EX´ o JY ra) 23
Expeditions 9, 11 — 13
Extinction 37, 51, 59

Feather stars 69
Feeding, dinosaurs 23
    fish 23
Finbacked reptiles 88, 89
Fins to legs 73 — 82
Fish 24, 73
    armoured 73, 75
    feeding 23
Flatworms 17
Flexicalymene (FLEX´ i ka LIM e nie) 48
Fly 24
"Forams" 39
    (Foraminifera)
Fossils, abundance 9, 13, 16, 35, 37, 38, 63, 68
    carbonized 15, 17, 18
    collecting 9, 11, 12, 13, 14, 25, 63, 65
    colour in 11, 68
    defined 9, 10
    frozen, 11
    impressions 11, 15, 18, 22
    petrified 9, 14, 15, 17, 19, 20, 22, 23, 24, 33
    preparation 12, 13, 14
    significance 13, 15, 16, 17, 18, 19 — 24, 30, 35
    variety 12, 13, 16, 35, 68
Fringe-fins 76 — 79, 80
Fungi (FUN jy) 17

Geologic section 25, 26, 27, 73, 85
Geologic time 10, 26, 27, 39, 49, 83
Gills 73
Gizzard stones 24
Granger, Walter 9, 63
Great Ice Age 10, 28
Green River, Utah 31
Ground sloths 21
Growth, fossils showing 20

Harpes (HAR peez) 49
Heart urchin 69
Helicoceras (hel i KOSS er as) 59, 60
Honeycomb coral 22
Horn-shells 52, 53, 54
    colours of 53, 56, 57
    cone-shaped 53, 54, 55, 56, 57
    Silurian 53
    straight 53, 55, 56
Horsetails 85, 88, 89
Hudsonaster (usually pronounced as if
    two words, Hudson and aster) 67
Hunters, snails 22
    vertebrates 22, 23, 90

Ice Age 10, 12, 72
Ichthyostega (IK´ thi o STEE ga) 79
Impressions 15
Index fossils 26, 27, 32
Ink bag 21, 61
Insects 81
Instinct, ancient 24
Isotelus 49
Jellyfish 16, 33, 35, 36
Jurassic (ju RASS ik) Period 28

Keyhole urchin 69

Lake deposits 31
Lamp-shells (brachiopods) 16, 20, 23,
    33, 36, 37
    Precambrian 33, 35
Lepidodendron (LEP´ i doe DEN
    dron) 84
Limestone, Indiana 39
Lingula (LING gu la) 37
Lituites (LIT yu EYE´ teez) 57, 59
Living chamber 53 – 56
Living Fossils 36, 69, 72
Lungfish 76

Mammoths 12, 18
Mastodons 21
Megistocrinus (me GISS´ toe KRY
    nus) evansi 66, 69
Mesozoic (MESS´ o ZO ik) Era 28
Miocene (MY o seen) Epoch 28
Mississippian Period 29, 62, 68

Mollusc shell 21, 22
Muscle scars 16, 18, 19, 22

Nautiloids (NAW ti loid) 52, 53, 54, 55
    ballast 54
    colour 53, 56, 57
    evolutionary changes 53, 54, 55, 56,
    57, 58, 61
    straight 53, 55, 56, 57
    uncoiled 56, 57, 59
Nautilus 24, 52, 53

Ogygopsis (O ji GOP´ sis) 45
Old Red Continent 73, 76, 85, 88
Old Red Sandstone 73, 76, 87
Olenellus (o le NEL us) 44, 45, 46, 47,
    49
Olenoides (o le NOY deez) 42
Oligocene (OLL i go seen) Epoch 28
Ordovician (OR´ doe vish un) Period
    29
    fossils 36, 37, 38, 70
    seas 36, 37, 38, 56, 68
Osteolepis (OS´ tee o LEP is) 76
Ostracoderm (os TRAK o derm) (an
    agnath) 74

Paleocene (PAY´ lee o SEEN) Epoch
28
Paleozoic (PAY´ lee o ZO ik) Era 50
Paradoxides (PAR´ a DOX i deez) 49
Pennsylvanian Period 29, 85
    end of
Pentremites (PEN tre MY´ teez) 66
Permian (PUR mi un) Period 10, 29, 68,
    85, 90
    amphibians 78 – 80, 81, 86
    reptiles 10, 80, 87
Petalocrinus (PET´ a lo KRY nus) 66
Petrified butterflies 33, 43
Petrified forest, Arizona
Petrified fossils 9, 14 – 17, 19 – 24, 33
Petrified nuts (blastoids)
Pleistocene (PLICE toe seen) Epoch 28
Pliocene (PLY o seen) Epoch 28
Precambrian Eras 29
    end 85
    fossils 33, 34

Preservation of fossils 39
Pteraspis (ter RAS pis) 75
Pygidium (pi JID i um)44, 45 — 47, 50

Quaternary (kwa TUR na ri) Period 28

Recent Epoch 28
Red Beds 10,
    fossils from 10
Reptiles, Pennsylvanian 80, 87, 88
    Permian 86, 88
    primitive 80, 86, 87 — 90
Restoration 13, 14, 19
Rocks, nature of 25 — 27, 32
Romer, Alfred S., on origin of 77
    amphibians 77 — 79, 81
    of reptiles 80, 81

Sand dollars 72
Scale trees 83, 84
Scaphites (ska FY teez if italicized;
    SKAF ites if not) 59, 60
Scouring rushes 84, 85
Sea buds (blastoids) 66, 68
Sea lilies (crinoids) 22, 63 — 67
Seas, ancient 37
Sea urchins 65, 69, 70 — 72
Seed ferns 85
Sensory systems 19
Septa 53 — 55, 57, 60, 61
Seymouria (see MOOR i ya) 80, 81, 82,
    87, 88
Sigillaria (SIJ´ i LAY ri uh) 84
Silurian (si LIU ri an) Period 29, 68
    fossils 52, 55
Siphuncle (SY fung kl) 55
Sizes, Permian reptiles 87 — 90
Skin-crusts 43, 44, 50
Snail 12, 20, 36, 37
    trails 21, 33

Sponge, limy, 33, 35, 36
Spores 18
Squids 21, 61, 62
Starfish 65, 67, 70 — 72
Stones, nature of 9 — 11
Stromatolites (STRO ma to lite) 34
Suture (SYU chur) 58, 60

Terataspis (TEHR´ a TASS pis) 47, 48,
    50, 51
Thaleops (THAL e ops) 49
Thorax 44 — 47, 51
Time scale 25, 26, 27, 28, 29, 33, 73
    building 25, 26, 27, 28, 29
Travel, by ancient animals
Tree ferns 83, 84
Triassic (try AS ik) Period 28, 58
Trilobites (TRY lo bite) 43 — 51, 52
    anatomy 17, 33, 43, 47, 49
    armour 43, 50
    egg-laying 47, 49
    enemies of 56
    enrolled 49, 50, 51
    evolution 43, 44, 45
    extinction 51
    feeding 47, 49
    habits 47, 50
    spiny 50
Turrilites (TUR´ i LY tees) 60

Uplift of marine deposits 40

Varanosaurus (VAR´ a no saw rus)87,
    88, 90

Weathering 31, 63, 64
Wood, petrified 16, 23
Worms, 17, 31, 47
    Precambrian 35

THE HOW AND WHY WONDER BOOK OF DINOSAURS   25p
552 86501 X

Dinosaurs ruled the prehistoric earth for a period of 120 million years. The full story of these fierce, forbidding and fascinating monsters is retold in the best-selling book of the *How and Why* series. Packed with illustrations, many in full colour, this book tells all there is to know about dinosaurs.

THE HOW AND WHY WONDER BOOK
   OF THE TOWER OF LONDON   20p
552 865451

The Tower of London is one of Britain's most famous historical buildings. Today it is known for the crown jewels and the world-famous 'Beefeaters'. In the past it has housed Kings and Queens, and served as a prison for Sir Walter Raleigh, the 'Little Princes', and other well known people. The full story of the Tower's past and present is retold in this book, with many illustrations.

THE HOW AND WHY WONDER BOOK
   OF EXTINCT ANIMALS   25p
552 865559

Here is a fabulous array of animals that have become extinct, from the early dinosaurs to more recent victims of man's actions. And there is also a warning: many species including pandas, tigers and leopards are in danger of disappearing, and the final question posed is 'Is the human race becoming extinct?'

HOW AND WHY WONDER BOOK
   OF THE HUMAN BODY   25p
552 86504 4

Knowledge of the human body's structure and functioning is essential for healthy living. Moreover, it is a fascinating field of study. Here is an informed and easy to read account of the body's working, reproduction, and how to maintain personal well-being. Illustrations enhance the text.

THE HOW AND WHY WONDER BOOK
   OF WILD ANIMALS   25p
552 86508 7

Information about many of the world's most interesting wild animals, what they look like, where they live, how they hunt, what they eat, their intelligence and means of protection — these are some of the features that make this book both educational and entertaining.

DANNY DUNN ON THE OCEAN FLOOR
by Jay Williams and Raymond Abrashkin   25p
552 52012 8   Carousel Fiction

In his second adventure, Danny Dunn and his friends Irene and Joe accompanied Professor Bullfinch and Dr Grimes to the seabed in their Bathyscape on a scientific quest. Danny took along his tape recorder to record the noises made by the fishes — and that's what started the trouble!

MYSTERY FOR ARCHIE by Robert Bateman   25p
552 52015 2   Carousel Fiction

When Archie volunteered for camera work on the film his school was making for a competition, he didn't expect any problems. But the camera disappeared before the film was completed and Archie was determined to find out who was trying to sabotage their entry. But time was beginning to run out ...

THE HOW AND WHY WONDER BOOK OF TIME   25p
552 86538 9

Do you know how men first learned to tell the time, or how an atomic clock works? This book tells you all about these and hundreds of other interesting facts on the measurement of time. Learn how to make your own waterclock or sandglass, too. This **How and Why Wonder Book** is packed with informative diagrams and illustrations.

THE GOD BENEATH THE SEA
by Leon Garfield and Edward Blishen   30p
552 52031 4   Carousel Fiction

This is one of the most important children's books since the war. Winner of the Carnegie Award for children's literature in 1970, and runner-up for the Kate Greenaway Medal, the book is a dramatic, forcefully poetic retelling of the classic Greek myths. It covers the creating of the Gods, the making of man, and the Gods' struggles to control man; into the vast canvas are woven a succession of myths such as the flood, Prometheus Sysphus and a multitude of others. This epoch-making book is supported by Charles Keeping's remarkable illustrations.

HERACLES THE STRONG by Ian Serraillier   25p
552 52034 9   Carousel Fiction

Heracles was the son of Zeus, the Father of the gods, but he was born into a mortal family. The goddess Hera hated Heracles because he was not her own, and in a fit of spite and jealousy drove him blindly mad. Like a whirlwind Heracles raged through the palace and committed the most dreadful crimes.

Condemned by the gods, Heracles had no alternative but to accept his punishment and tackle the twelve seemingly impossible tasks set before him by the cowardly King Eurystheus.

THE STORY OF BRITAIN by R. J. Unstead   30p
Series   Carousel Non-Fiction.

A country is forged by its history, the battles and intrigues of by-gone
ages laying the foundations of today. From its beginnings as an island to
the end of the Second World War, this series is the record of the men
and women who played a role in shaping the character of England
now. It traces the emergence of England as a nation.

EVERYDAY LIFE IN PREHISTORIC TIMES
by Marjorie and C.B.H. Quennell   25p
Series   Carousel Non-Fiction

This series presents a picture of how our forefathers lived in their
prehistoric world, moving out of their caves into the earliest
settlements; discovering metals; making fires; building and
constructing the first organised villages. The EVERYDAY LIFE series
follows them, detailing their development into civilization as we know
it.

LOOKING AND FINDING by Geoffrey Grigson   25p
552 54007 2   Carousel Non-Fiction

You can find sunken treasure, hidden away in some long-forgotten
shipwreck, or discover the past through scattered fossils and ancient
inscriptions. It depends what you're looking for, how you go about
finding it. It depends where you're looking, how you go about getting
there. But once the search begins there's no knowing what you might
stumble across.

20th CENTURY DISCOVERY:
    THE STRUCTURE OF LIFE by Isaac Asimov   25p
552 54012 9   Carousel Non-Fiction

20th CENTURY DISCOVERY:
    THE PLANETS by Isaac Asimov   25p
552 54013 7   Carousel Non-Fiction

Dr Asimov's books recount the major events of scientific discovery in
this century: how the atom has been investigated and its power
harnessed; how delicate the balance of nature is; and how, through his
examination of the structure of life, man may have come close to the
artificial creation of life itself; how the development of different
telescopes has enabled man to observe the stars and planets, how he has
calculated their age and distance, and how the development of space
travel has affected our knowledge of the Universe.
Illustrated with photographs.

EVERDAY LIFE IN THE VIKING AGE
by Jacqueline Simpson   30p
552 54011 0   Carousel Non-Fiction

The Vikings were not merely plunderers and marauders, but also a
civilised people with a culture of their own — as recent excavations
have shown. Jacqueline Simpson provides a full and fascinating
account of their way of life covering their domestic life as well as their
better-known overseas adventures.

If you would like to receive a newsletter telling you about our new children's books, fill in the coupon with your name and address and send it to:

Gillian Osband, Transworld Publishers Ltd.,

57-59 Uxbridge Road, Ealing, London, W5

- - - - - - - - - - - - - - - - - - -

Name ....

Address ....

....

....

CHILDRENS NEWSLETTER